THE
GOVERNOR'S LADY
Mrs. Philip Gidley King

THE
GOVERNOR'S LADY

MRS. PHILIP GIDLEY KING

*An Australian
Historical Narrative
by*
MARNIE BASSETT

MELBOURNE UNIVERSITY PRESS

First published, 1940, by
Oxford University Press, London
Second edition, 1956
Reissued as an Australian Paperbound, 1961, by
Melbourne University Press, Carlton,
Victoria, Australia
Reprinted 1992 by
The Book Printer, Victoria, for
Melbourne University Press

This book is copyright. Apart from any fair dealing for the purposes of private study, research, criticism or review, as permitted under the Copyright Act, no part may be reproduced by any process without written permission. Enquiries should be made to the publisher.

© *Ian Basset 1992*
© *Jenny Young 1992*

National Library of Australia Cataloguing-in-Publication entry

Bassett, Marnie, 1889–1980.
The governor's lady. Mrs Philip Gidley King.
2nd ed.
Biblography.
Includes index.
ISBN 0 522 84499 5.

1. King, Anna Josepha, 1765–1844. 2. King, Philip Gidley, 1758–1808. 3. Governors—New South Wales—Wives—Biography. I. Title.
994.402092

To
D. O. M.
and
W. E. B.

Acknowledgements

My grateful thanks are due to the Trustees of the Mitchell Library, Sydney, for permission to publish pictures and extracts from manuscripts in their possession, and especially to Miss Ida Leeson, Chief Librarian, and Miss Monica Flower, of the Manuscript Room, for much sympathetic help.

I wish also to thank Mr. C. A. McCallum, of the Historical Section, and the other members of the Staff of the Melbourne Public Library for helpfulness at all times.

I acknowledge my high indebtedness to Miss S. Macarthur Onslow of Menangle, New South Wales, and to the Misses Macarthur King of Sydney for the loan of manuscripts; to Sir Philip Goldfinch of Sydney, Dr. Keith Brown of Parramatta, and the Misses Chapman of Frankston, Victoria, for permission to reproduce pictures in their possession; and to my brother, Dr. J. I. O. Masson, F.R.S., who corrected the proofs.

M. B.

Contents

I. NEW HOLLAND	1
II. NORFOLK ISLAND	20
III. STANDING BY	35
IV. RETURN TO SYDNEY	43
V. LIFE IN THE COLONY	55
VI. FRIENDS, FEUDS, AND FOREIGNERS	77
VII. EXILED IN ENGLAND: AUSTRALIA AT LAST	95

APPENDIXES

1. THE CHILDREN OF GOVERNOR KING	111
2. THE KINGS, SOME LAND, AND THE WILD CATTLE	118
3. BIBLIOGRAPHY	122
INDEX	124

Author's Note

This story is authentic throughout. Most of the facts, and many of the passages quoted, are to be found in contemporary documents published in the *New South Wales Historical Records*. To avoid overweighting the text with footnotes, reference to the exact volume and page of the *Records* has been omitted, but in every instance they are my authority where no other source is acknowledged.

M. B.

MRS. PHILIP GIDLEY KING
Miniature; artist and date unknown
By permission of the Trustees of the Mitchell Library, Sydney

LIEUT. PHILIP GIDLEY KING
in 1789

CHAPTER I

New Holland

1788–1791

It is sometimes difficult, in this life that is built on a scaffolding of quick communications, expert medical services, and domestic labour-saving appliances, to realize what existence must have meant to the women who came to Australia in the very earliest days. Contemporary official accounts refer to them hardly at all; they are there by implication only, and when we have read all we can in the printed records of the adventures of those days, adventures in which they shared, they still remain elusive shadows behind the solid forms of their husbands. Fortunately, however, there exist a few manuscript diaries and letters and a few rare books that, combined with the official records, help us to uncover something of the story of these women and give us at least a partial realization of what their lives were like. They endured so much, and we almost owe it to them to find out all that we can.

One such story is that of Mrs. King, the first woman to come to Australia as a governor's wife. For its earliest chapter we have to go back to the days when Australia was called New Holland; when George III, temporarily recovered from his insanity, was at the height of his popularity, and Louis XVI, still King, no longer ruled France. Navigators were satisfying their passion for exploration, regardless of the growing turmoil in Europe; the young Beethoven was delighting Mozart with his playing in Vienna; Caroline Herschel in England was discovering her comets, sweeping the Heavens with a telescope even smaller than her tiny self;

and Jane Austen, still in her teens, was watching the provincial world about her and making reflections just as valuable as those of Edmund Burke.

It was from that provincial world that our Governor's Lady came, and it would be hard to imagine a less suitable preparation for the life she was to lead. 'Young ladies', says Mr. Woodhouse, 'should take care of themselves. Young ladies are delicate plants. They should take care of their health and their complexion. My dear, did you change your stockings?' This to a young friend who had run a message in a sprinkle of rain. Throughout Jane Austen's novels, younger and less apprehensive men than Mr. Woodhouse are constantly concerned to save the fair sex from colds, fatigue, and any exertion greater than a short walk in fine weather on a perfect road. Mentally, they are not expected to be any more daring. They might never have heard of discontent in England or of revolution in France. The young, genteel, and unmarried females—the Elizabeths, the Catherines, the Emmas, and the Janes—passed their time in activity over very small things, or in doing nothing at all.

Jane Austen drew people as they were. Anna Josepha Coombe, of Hatherleigh in Devonshire, had she not married, might have been as these, with no task harder than matching a skein of silk, no experience more stirring than the advent of new neighbours or an occasional rout. Had she married a farmer or an attorney, or a small tradesman, Devon might have bounded her horizon all her days. But in 1791, when she was twenty-six, she married an officer in the Royal Navy; adventure seized her and took her out of England—reality came to her with a rush.

Anna Josepha's husband was a Cornishman, Lieut. Philip Gidley King, aged thirty-three, and her own first cousin. Of undistinguished origin—he was the son of a

NEW HOLLAND

draper—he seems to have been better educated than many naval men of his day. He had just recently returned from an adventurous mission entrusted to His Majesty's naval officers—the establishment of the convict settlement at Port Jackson, in New South Wales. He had been chosen for this by Captain Arthur Phillip, whose terrible task it had been to convey a thousand people across the world, to land them on an unknown shore, and there, remote from all help, to build some sort of community out of the miserable material from England's prisons and hulks. Phillip chose King because he knew and trusted him—they had already seen service together; and it was to King that he delegated the special task of establishing a sub-colony on Norfolk Island, a thousand miles from the New South Wales coast. In February 1788, less than a month after the arrival of the First Fleet, King had been dispatched from Port Jackson with a handful of convicts—men and women—a few free men, a small guard, some farm-yard animals, and provisions for six months; and there, while Phillip struggled with the horrors of Sydney's first months, King, lonely in his surf-bound craggy little dominion, tackled his similar problems on a diminutive scale. He had done well, and now late in 1790 had arrived in London, sent by Phillip to report personally to the Government on the true state and urgent needs of the penal settlement. And evidently, in the intervals of waiting on Lord Grenville and Mr. Under-Secretary Nepean and satisfying the scientific curiosity of Sir Joseph Banks, he found time for more personal matters, for in March 1791, just after being promoted to Commander, he and Anna Josepha were married at St. Martin-in-the-Fields. It was all done in a distressing hurry; he had been only a few weeks in England, and was actually ill in bed, when he received unexpected orders to sail almost at once. He had been appointed Lieutenant-Governor of Norfolk Island, so that she knew that marriage to him meant at least a temporary good-bye to England: whether she married him because of or in spite of this we shall never know.

Did King tell his wife-to-be the truth about the settlement at Sydney Cove? It is to be hoped that he did. In those days there was a different point of view about the rights of the social outcast; but King was a merciful man, and he probably did describe in more or less true colours that voyage three years before, when the transports set sail laden between their dark decks with the seven hundred odd convicts, some old, mostly half-clothed, and numbers already enfeebled by long confinement in filthy prisons or hulks. He must have told her of their arrival in a harbour where no ship had sheltered before, and where a thousand people, with no preparation and few tools and negligible skill, without health or hope, had been landed in the woods at the water's edge to build for themselves a habitation in the wilderness. He is certain to have spoken much of his friend, Governor Arthur Phillip, the man whose courage, humanity, and common sense had brought them to that anchorage without disaster, and whom King had left some months ago trying to make a settlement without the proper means to shelter, clothe, or feed the inhabitants. When King sailed from Port Jackson, the Governor and the marines, the convicts and the free women who were the convicts' wives, the children, and the one and only free man were still subsisting on reduced rations of the salt pork that they had brought from England eighteen months before, supplemented by unreliable supplies of fish and the luxury of an occasional kangaroo. Ministers, never very ardent in the affairs of the Botany Bay expedition that they had hoped to be allowed to forget once the Fleet left Spithead, had larger matters to think of than victualling convicts in the Antipodes. King had been sent home to make clear to them why the settlement was not yet self-supporting, why they must have regular shipments of provisions, of boots and blankets, spades, frying-pans, and hospital supplies. And as an honest man—and he was a very honest man—he will not have kept his descriptions entirely for Ministers and Under-Secretaries; he must have told his Anna Josepha at least something of the facts. King, however, would not have been human if he had not put another and contrasting picture in front of his bride: that of the little Pacific island measuring a few miles each way, steep and wooded, where she was to make her home; where the soil was rich, the water plentiful, the climate delightful. Isolated? Yes, admitted: but who wants Paradise to be too accessible? There may even have been attraction in its very inaccessibility, its remoteness from the clouds gathering in Europe, a suggestion of Arcadia—at least to the two who were to be ruler and consort, if not to those banished there to be subjects against their will.

There was something else about which one feels that Captain King must have dealt openly with his bride, for it was to concern her very closely for the next few years. Six convict women of good character had been included in the first settlement party sent to Norfolk Island; with one of them King had tempered his loneliness, and by her had two sons.[1] This was only in accordance with the custom of his day: many officers then and later lived openly with female companions listed quaintly in the official records as concubines. What does distinguish King from many of his contemporaries is the responsible and affectionate feeling he evidently had for the children of such a union. But, even in the eighteenth century, for a bride to be faced with family

[1] Appendix I.

responsibilities ready-made, and from such an origin, must have been a test of good nature and good sense. It is to Mrs. King's credit that from the earliest days of her marriage she helped her husband to care for these two boys, who during King's lifetime had their share of his meagre salary as well as of his generous love.

Had King always known his cousin, with her valuable qualities of practical sense and good spirits, and planned during the voyage from New Holland to ask her to return to help him with his difficult life? Or did he, as one family tradition has it, propose to her at a ball at their first meeting and marry her two days later just before they embarked? The first seems the more likely: but whether he acted on impulse or by design, in desperation or at the inspiration of romantic love, she turned out to be the very wife for him.

In March 1791, immediately after her wedding, Mrs. King set sail in H.M.S. *Gorgon* on the first of her adventures in the New World.[1] Only her husband's entreaties to Lord Grenville had saved them from travelling in a convict ship. She was now, in a small way, an important person; we have to guess what she wore on this important day. A cloak over a full-skirted dress of cloth with a buffon of gauze around her shoulders, a broad-brimmed hat with a feather, her dark hair probably without powder, according to the new fashion, and curled all over her head, falling on her shoulders; her feet in high-heeled shoes, her hands hidden in a muff. On later voyages she was to write the diaries that can be read in the Mitchell Library, but of the *Gorgon* voyage there is no description from her own pen. There were, however, two of the ship's company who help us to see life as it was lived in the *Gorgon*, and give us little pictures of Mrs. King her-

---

[1] They were married at St. Martin-in-the-Fields on March 11th, and sailed from Spithead on March 15th, 1791.

self: one of these was the sprightly Mrs. Parker, wife of the officer commanding the ship, who published a book after her return to England,[1] and the other was the seventeen-year-old William Chapman, a protégé of Governor Phillip, who wrote delicious letters to his Honoured Mother and to Sister Fanny, fortunately treasured through the years.[2]

It is strange to us to hear of officers' wives travelling in a man-of-war, but in the eighteenth century it was often done, and, if not positively allowed by the Admiralty, very liberally winked at. There was, for instance, in Jane Austen's *Persuasion*, Mrs. Croft, that perfect picture of the comradely wife, who had a

'reddened and weather-beaten complexion, the consequence of her having been almost as much at sea as her husband,' the Admiral.

' "What a great traveller you must have been ma'am!" said Mrs. Musgrove to Mrs. Crofts.

"Pretty well, ma'am, in the fifteen years of my marriage; though many women have done more. I have crossed the Atlantic four times, and have been once to the East Indies and back again, and only once; besides being in different places about home: Cork, and Lisbon, and Gibraltar. But I never went beyond the Straits, and never was in the West Indies. We do not call Bermuda, or Bahama, you know, the West Indies"

'Mrs. Musgrove had not a word to say in dissent; she could not accuse herself of having ever called them anything in the whole course of her life.

' "And I do assure you ma'am", pursued Mrs. Croft, "that nothing can exceed the accommodations of a man-of-war; I speak, you know, of the higher rates. When you come to a frigate, of course, you are more confined; though any reasonable woman may be perfectly happy in one of them; and I can safely say, that the happiest part of my life has been spent on board a ship." '

[1] *Voyage around the World in the 'Gorgon' Man of War.*
[2] *Chapman Papers.*

But even to a naval wife of those days a voyage to New Holland must have been a different matter. Here is what Mrs. Mary Ann Parker has to say of the opportunity that came to her just as her husband was about to leave with his ship as escort to the Third Fleet of convict transports going to the other end of the world. The *Gorgon* was, she says, then at Portsmouth, refitting for her intended voyage to New South Wales, and exchanging the provisions she then had for the newest and best in store,

'when it was proposed to me to accompany Captain Parker in the intended expedition to New Holland. A fortnight was allowed me for my decision. An indulgent husband waited my answer at Portsmouth; I did not therefore take a moment's consideration, but, by return of post, forwarded one perfectly consonant to his request, and my most sanguine wishes—that of going with him to the remotest parts of the globe; although my considerate readers will naturally suppose that my feelings were somewhat wounded at the thoughts of being so long absent from two dear children, and a mother, with whom I had travelled into France, Italy and Spain; and from whom I had never been separated a fortnight in the whole course of my life.'

Before sailing finally from Spithead they 'received on board Captain Gidley King of the Royal Navy, the intended Lieutenant-Governor of Norfolk Island in the Pacific Ocean, together with Mrs. King'.

'After a fortnight's seasoning and buffeting in the channel', Mrs. Parker is able to state, 'I began to enjoy the voyage I had undertaken; and with the polite attention of the officers on board, and my amiable companion Mrs. King, we glided over many a watery grave with peace of mind, and uninterrupted happiness....'

They followed the usual route by way of Teneriffe and St. Jago in the Cape Verde Islands to the Cape of Good

Hope. At Teneriffe there was no salute to H.M. King George's ship, as orders from Spain forbade such compliments to foreign ships of war, but what was lacking in formal ceremonial was made up in friendly and colourful hospitality, and the ladies evidently had the time of their lives. There had been 'tedious calms' on the way to Teneriffe; now came an exciting interlude of dinners and picnics, donkey rides, gifts of fruits and salads, visits to the admiring wives of Spanish officials and to the attentive bachelor members of the English business community. Every one was very gracious, and Mrs. Parker was able to act as interpreter, having lived three years in Spain—indeed, Mrs. Parker is not a little complacent about her foreign accomplishments, and one cannot help feeling that Mrs. King's nose was slightly out of joint. Here also Mrs. King had a bad fright, for her husband, says Chapman, had a very terrible fall from a staircase, injuring an arm and nearly killing himself.

Ten days they frolicked at the feet of the almighty Peak, and then sailed for St. Jago. Sharks were caught at sea, and the men, but not the ladies, ate the tails of the youngest. The ship ran into squally weather, and Mrs. Parker says that 'the noise made by the working of the vessel, and the swinging of the glass shades that held our lights, rendered the cabin very dismal'. Once it was so rough that they had to dine on the deck of the cabin, 'but these little difficulties were scarcely felt, the party being in good humour, and our spirits being well supported by good broth, roast pig, and plumb-puddings—thanks to my caterer, who had so well provided for so long a voyage'.

At St. Jago, they fell in with four of the transports to whom they were acting as convoy, and made the acquaintance of two people whose lives were for many years to be woven closely with the Kings'—Captain Paterson of the New South Wales Corps, and his lady, on their way to Port Jackson. Here they treated themselves with coconuts and pineapples and stocked the ship with fruit, poultry, and goats.

Towards the end of June they could count their long voyage half over. At this time of year, Mrs. Parker says, sudden hurricanes sweep round the mountains of Southern Africa and make the Bay at Capetown 'too dangerous to risk a vessel at', so the *Gorgon* anchored in the safety of Simon's Bay. A letter from Captain King to Mr. Peter de Witt, merchant, brought him to wait upon them, and also two carriages to convey the party to the Cape.

'Eager for a little shore amusement,' says Mrs. Parker, 'we rose early, and after breakfasting upon rolls and such fruit as we had procured from the Bay, Lieutenant Governor King, Mrs. King, our first Lieutenant, Captain Parker and myself went on shore, the port saluting with fifteen guns, and our ship returning the compliment with an equal number. I could not help being well pleased at finding myself once more safe landed.'

They bade a temporary good-bye to the *Gorgon* and

'set off for Cape Town, Captain King and Mr. de Witt in the chaise and four, and the rest of us in the carriage drawn with eight horses, somewhat resembling a covered waggon, except having seats within, and little gaudy decorations'.

The road was joltingly disagreeable, and they were thankful to stop the horses and pause for dinner at a Government half-way house. On the way they passed parties of soldiers marching to Simon's Bay to embark there for Batavia to replace others who had died from the malignant fever that made that island a place to dread.

At last they reached the foot of Table Mountain 'most completely jostled and tired'. In those days there were no hotels at the Cape, and they lodged with the mother of the merchant, Mr. Peter de Witt.

'She received us with much complacency,' says Mrs. Parker, 'and immediately procured us a little cargo of bread and butter, which I believe we all relished very much, having had no overplus of that article during our passage. The countenance of the good lady was pleasing, her manner engaging, and her motherly attention, during our short *séjour* at her habitation, such as I shall ever remember with the greatest degree of satisfaction.'

Eating Mrs. de Witt's salt, however, does not prevent Mrs. Parker from saying some very naughty things about Mrs. de Witt's figure, which she likens to a Dutch man-of-war. That night she sleeps comfortably in a bed that does not rock, and wakes 'particularly thankful to Providence'. She says her prayers and goes to look out of the window and—horror! What does she see but the remains of the ship *Guardian*, wrecked recently on her way to Port Jackson with stores! She thinks of that dreadful iceberg that struck the ship one foggy morning, leaving her rudderless and waterlogged four hundred leagues from the Cape; of the chance that brought across her track a Dutch ship from the Spice Islands, whose men helped her to struggle back to port under her gallant commander, Riou. She takes a long look at the *Guardian*'s remains—then wisely decides not to think of the possibility of a similar fate for the *Gorgon*, and hastens to her companions and the comfort of a large breakfast handed round by slaves.

The day turned out wet, and the ladies, separated from their baggage, had nothing to wear. They received calls from the Dutch Governor—that reluctant Mynheer van Graaf, from whom Phillip and King had with difficulty extracted supplies for the Fleet and the Settlement in 1788—and 'Colonel Burrington of the Bengal Army' and other gentlemen (alas! where was the baggage with their fresh frocks?).

In the next few days the hospitality of Teneriffe was repeated, with English and Dutchmen instead of English and Spaniards for hosts, and with a background of work for the men of the party, who had to obtain from an unwilling Governor supplies for New South Wales and to get the fruit-trees and livestock safe on board. Mrs. Parker notes that Capetown has 'no public amusements or any particular promenades', and attributes the remarkable bulk of the women to 'their going without stays and sitting much in the house with their feet continually lifted on a chair'. She informs us that 'the Churches at Cape Town are open at eight in the morning, when the genteel classes go in Sedan chairs, which are usually kept in the entrance to their houses'.

The baggage arrived from Simon's Bay, and there was dining and dancing to regimental bands, and more feasting and more dancing, but though 'surrounded with novelties and amusements' Mrs. Parker thought of the *Guardian* wreck and could not forget the peril of her husband who had gone to bring the *Gorgon* round to Table Bay. He arrived, and when some of the transports anchored in Simon's Bay the party was completed by Captain and Mrs. Paterson, who stayed under the same elastic roof. While the ladies King and Paterson and Parker revelled in the moonlit nights, the music and the feastings, did they sometimes think of those nine hundred miserable wretches imprisoned between decks over in Simon's Bay? From later knowledge of the kindness of Mrs. King, one feels that she, at least, must have spared for them an occasional pitying thought.

During the *Gorgon's* visit to Table Bay, there arrived two ships homeward bound with tea from China after deliver-

NEW HOLLAND

ing their loads of convicts at Sydney Cove. These were the *Neptune*, of black reputation, and the *Lady Juliana*, both of the Second Fleet of convict transports. They were full of disquieting reports on the food problem in the settlement, and of how anxiously the Governor had been awaiting the arrival of the *Gorgon* months before. Captain Parker longed to be off. The loading was finished at last, the animals and the fruit-trees were safely stowed. They set sail on the last day of July, and the de Witt family came in a body to see them off.

'We returned', says Mrs. Parker, 'to our little sea amusements in peace and tranquillity of mind. With my companion, Mrs. King, and the society of the ship, I seldom, if ever, found anything unpleasant, except the pitching of the ship which motion proved very disagreeable to me to the end of our voyage.'

Mrs. King, we are told (but by young Chapman, not by Mrs. Parker), was never seasick at all—in that respect at least Mrs. King outdid that leading lady, the Captain's wife.

Travellers to Australia by the Cape route know the grey skies and huge seas of the Southern Indian Ocean into which the *Gorgon* now sailed. It was in these gloomy regions that she met with deaths from illness and accident. William Chapman, on his way to Norfolk Island to serve under Captain King, wrote to his mother with the nonchalance of seventeen years, 'We have had but five deaths since we left England.' He described how, with Mrs. King, he was in Captain King's cabin sitting on the stern lockers when he heard a shout and looked out and saw a man's hat carried past the window. He cried out and Mrs. King looked and saw the hat, and then they saw a man, and 'it frightened Mrs. King very much'. The man was a ship's carpenter. A cutter was lowered, but the seas were too rough for rescue, and in hoisting the boat up another man was lost. 'A dismal sky and a deluge of rain concluded this disastrous and eventful night' says the elegant pen of Mrs. Parker.

At last, on the 11th of September, they sighted the coast of New Holland. On the 17th, expecting to arrive at Port Jackson the next day, they gathered festively with the officers of the wardroom at what was intended to be a farewell dinner, but perverse winds blew them away from the coast once more. On the 19th they again sighted land; by sunset they were thwarted again by torrents of rain, thunder, and lightning, and a fireball that seemed to rend the ship. At midnight the weather cleared and Mrs. Parker pondered on the 'satisfaction' that their delayed arrival was going to cause. 'My pen', she says, 'is utterly incompetent to the task of describing our feelings on this occasion.' It is certain that by this time Mrs. King's at least must have been beyond description.

While the *Gorgon* was battling to arrive, Sydney was longing for the *Gorgon*. When more than a year ago King had sailed for Batavia in the Colony's only ship to send back food and make his way thence to England as best he might, he had left behind him in the empty harbour a feeling almost of despair. Since then ships had indeed come, but had brought more new inhabitants than provisions, and the settlement had suffered from hunger and drought, from dysentery and scurvy, from quarrelling and thieving—from hunger above all. The *Gorgon*, bringing supplies, was believed to be on her way long before she had left Spithead. From the South Head of Port Jackson the look-out watched the empty ocean; from the settlement anxious eyes turned constantly to the signal station on South Head. An officer's wife in Sydney Cove wrote to a friend in England to describe the feelings of the Colony at the non-arrival of the 'so long wished for and so long expected' ship. This was

Elizabeth Macarthur, wife of Lieut. John Macarthur of the New South Wales Corps, who had arrived with her husband in June 1790 with the ill-famed Second Fleet. Mrs. Macarthur's letter was dated a few days before the *Gorgon* left England. She described how even before then

'week after week stole away and month after month with little diversity. Each succeeding sunset produced among us wild and vague conjectures of what could be the *Gorgon*'s delay, and still we remained unsatisfied—indeed, all our surmises have nearly worn themselves out, and we are at a loss for new ones. . . .'[1]

The delay was due simply to an official change of plan: but now at long last the *Gorgon* was safely anchored inside the Heads.[2]

Captain King was only a passenger, so that as the ship beat up the harbour next morning he was free to stand with his wife on the deck and point out to her all the places that he knew—the wooded slopes, the little islands, the beach where fish were netted, the bay where rushes were cut for thatching roofs; in the Cove itself the lines of convict huts and the soldiers' quarters near the Tank Stream that was the settlement's only fresh water; the stores where flour and rice and pork were guarded as though they were the crown jewels; the Commandant's brick house, the observatory on the hill, and on the slope above the Cove the unpretentious Government House with 'the only pair of stairs in the Colony'. Together the Kings must have watched 'the uncommon manners' of the natives paddling their canoes about the ship, while Mrs. Parker tossed them ribbons, and the crowds of people of all sorts who gathered rejoicing on the shore to greet the vessel as she dropped anchor at the end of her six months' voyage.

They had arrived, and famine was postponed. The Kings

[1] *The Macarthurs of Camden*, pp. 494–507.
[2] *Account of the English Colony in New South Wales*, p. 178.

walked up to Government House to stay with Governor Phillip; the Parkers remained on board. The Governor celebrated with a dinner-party, where no doubt Mrs. King and Mrs. Parker were excused from the rationed Colony's rule—hitherto relaxed only for Mrs. Macarthur, the sole lady on the Government House dinner-lists—that guests must bring their own bread. Was it on that day that they ate the dish described to his mother by William Chapman—'a pye called Bowow Pye made of native dog and very good it was'? It may well have been at this party that they first tasted 'part of a kingaroo' skilfully dressed by the Governor's French chef, which Mrs. Parker says she ate 'with much glee'. . . . A chef, candlelight and mahogany, silks and epaulettes, news of friends, talk of Europe: and outside, huddled between the meagre trees and the water's edge, the crude beginnings of a future in which few but the indomitable Phillip believed.

The ladies met almost daily at Government House after breakfast and at frequent picnics, at which they drank from the 'tea equipage' on the turf, were all admiration of the strange birds and flowering shrubs, all delight at feasts of oysters arranged round the hat brims of the *Gorgon's* crew. Mrs. Macarthur was invited to join these excursions—Mrs. Macarthur, who had been thirsting for congenial feminine company, 'having no female friend to unbend to, nor a single woman with whom I could converse with any satisfaction to myself, the clergyman's wife being a person in whose society I could reap neither profit nor pleasure'. Poor Mrs. Revd. Johnson—slain with a sniff! Mrs. Macarthur fortunately found Mrs. Parker 'very amiable and intelligent' and Mrs. King (more guardedly) 'possessed of a great share of good nature and frankness', and she wrote that 'our little circle of late has been quite brilliant'. The clergyman himself sometimes made one of the picnic parties: did his wife, busy with her children, look with longing from the door of her thatched hut at the 'brilliant circle' setting off in boats to dine out 'under an awning on some pleasant point of land?'

There was another side to the Watteau-like picture conveyed by polite feminine raptures on these Antipodean *fêtes-champêtres*. The transports of the Third Fleet were arriving in ones and twos, most of them unhealthy ships. Two hundred convicts had died on the voyage, hundreds more were now unloaded, and the makeshift hospital overflowed with the sick and dying. Riotous sailors bringing spirits ashore from the transports made conditions uglier still. Not Watteau, but Hogarth, might have painted the settlement then. And indeed Mrs. Parker herself writes in horror of the scenes she saw when she visited the hospital, and she roundly condemns the methods of transporting the convicts at so much a head whether delivered alive in Sydney or not.

On the anniversary of King George III's accession to the throne, the *Gorgon* dressed ship and fired a salute of twenty-one guns, while the Governor entertained all the naval and military officers in the Colony—more than fifty—to dinner. Mrs. Parker says that the Governor's

'unremitting attention to his guests' rendered the day very agreeable, 'could we have forgotten that it was the eve of our separation from Captain King and his lady, whose affability had so much contributed to the pleasantry of our voyage thus far; and who, with Captain and Mrs. Paterson and several other military officers destined for Norfolk Island, set sail the next day, accompanied to the end of the Cove by the Governor, Judge-Advocate, Captain Parker and many others who were anxious to be in their company as long as possible'.

It is time to say good-bye to Mrs. Parker and follow Mrs.

King. The *Gorgon*—'our happy bark'—sailed soon after for England, carrying amongst other things a kangaroo for King George.

At the Cape they were 'gratified with the company of Captain Edwards of His Majesty's ship *Pandora*', lately wrecked, the captor of a number of the *Bounty* mutineers and surely, despite Mrs. Parker's gratification, one of the most inhuman men in sea-history. Mrs. Parker adds that the convicts lately escaped from Port Jackson also embarked in the *Gorgon* at the Cape. These were the romantic Mary Bryant and the four surviving men who with her had sailed in a fishing-boat from Sydney to Coupang and were now returning to England to face another trial. These runaways and the unhappy *Bounty* mutineers, all brought aboard by Captain Edwards, and all, including Edwards, survivors of open-boat voyages of unequalled peril and length, must have been as tragic and adventurous a party as ever came together between the decks of one ship.

The *Gorgon*, complete with the kangaroo, reached the coasts of England only fifteen months after she had left them on her voyage around the world. Captain Parker landed his dispatches at St. Helen's, and it was Captain Edwards who accompanied Mrs. Parker on shore at Portsmouth. 'After four hours rowing against wind and tide, we landed at the Salley-Port, where we were met by many who [were] astonished at the speedy return of our ship.'

Poor Mrs. Parker now learned that her boy had died while his parents were at sea. 'This vacancy in my family', she naïvely says, 'did not remain long after my arrival', for a few days after she landed another son was born in lodgings in Frith Street, Soho. Soon afterwards Mrs. Parker found herself a widow. Her book was written in an attempt to earn money for her family, the youngest of whom, she says, was on her left arm most of the time that her right was busy with her pen. One hopes that the judicious dedication to the Princess of Wales, and the list of genteel subscribers, brought poor Mrs. Parker a useful sum. It is of interest that among the names of subscribers from Bath is that of the brilliant and then famous lady of letters, Hannah More.

CHAPTER II

Norfolk Island

1791-1796

AT long last, Mrs. King had embarked on the final stage of her journey. Another week, and their ship, the *Atlantic*, was off the Island waiting for the wind to drop so that a boat could get safely through the surf. Governor Phillip thought it 'one of the finest islands in the world', but it was so difficult of access that the French navigator Lapérouse and his officers, who had been unable to land there, described it as fit only for angels and eagles to live on. Mrs. King had heard a great deal about that surf, and dreaded it. Young William Chapman, who had become devoted to his Chief's wife on the passage out, had guessed the special reason for her anxiety and mentioned it to his mother. 'I wish she was safe landed', he wrote, 'the sooner the better'. Mrs. King was in fact expecting her first baby in a few weeks. It is a relief to know of a surgeon's being aboard, and Mrs. Paterson to play the part of female friend.

On the day that the ship hove in sight of the Island, a marine officer resident there recorded in his diary 'cloudy weather' and 'a great surf'; next day, fine weather and a good deal of surf; the following morning fine weather and no surf, wind from the northward. 'After breakfast,' he says, 'Captain King and lady, with Captain Peterson [sic] and lady, came on shore. Mrs. King appears to be a genteel woman, not very pretty, and Mrs. Peterson a good cosy Scotch lass and fit for a soldier's wife.' The writer, be it noted, was a soldier.[1]

[1] *Journal of Lieut. R. Clark.*

Mrs. King was no eagle, and though young Chapman considered her almost an angel—she was so good, he said, that it was a pleasure for any person to be near her—it must have been a very human and thankful woman that stepped ashore on that morning in November 1791. This little pine-clad world, remote in the Pacific Ocean, was to be her home for the next five years. Here she was to face the troubles that come to most married women—illness, money worries, concern for her husband's difficulties and his health, and for the well-being of her children—and she had to face them without the aids of civilization; but on that day, perhaps, she was without foreboding, ready to enjoy the adventure begun at the altar of St. Martin-in-the-Fields.

The settlement, Sydney Bay, was on the south side of the island, where the precipitous cliffs gave way to a gentler coast-line. Behind, the steep hills were dark with giant pines; in front lay spread the glory of the Pacific Ocean, as blue and green and glittering as the fan of a peacock's tail. Spray from the surf blew in at the windows of the sombre little buildings grouped on a clearing near the rocky shore. A road led inland and across the Island to two other tiny towns, each with its hundred convicts and its corporal's guard. The hilly island was laced with streams and much of it was covered with impenetrable wood, shelter for owls, doves, hawks, parrots, and many smaller birds; a kind of rat was the only wild animal to be found, nor in this Eden were there any snakes. In the clearings there were plantations of wheat and indian corn, and in the valleys were grazing grounds for the little flocks of sheep and goats and poultry and for the precious swine that, salted or fresh, were the staple food of the Island. In that sub-tropical climate vines and sugar-cane flourished already, and there were a few oranges and lemons; other fruit trees, brought from the

Cape in the *Gorgon*, were to be planted out by King when the right time came.

On the Sunday after the arrival of the Lieutenant-Governor, the garrison and the other inhabitants gathered in front of Government House to hear King's Commission read. There were about a thousand people altogether. With the Commandant, Major Ross, and his marines, who were to return to Sydney to embark in the *Gorgon* for England, were King, the only man in the blue and gold of the Navy, and a handful of officers and men in the scarlet and white of the New South Wales Corps. There were half-a-dozen civilian officers, wigged and ruffled, and there was the Rev. Richard Johnson of Cambridge University in sober black. With Mrs. King was Mrs. Paterson, their cloaks and feathers not quite so fine as when they had left London nearly a year before, but none the less the envy of the garrison wives. Drawn up in rows were the eight hundred convicts, men and women, dressed in the drab remnants of their own or government clothing; nearby, the overseers and a few free settlers, no different in appearance from the convicts, however greater the grace they felt within. And with all these men and women, there by choice or by compulsion, were the involuntary camp-followers of England's penal army overseas, the hundred children of the settlement, called from their play to stand in their rags for a solemn half-hour, until three concluding cheers for His Majesty should release them again to their pool-paddling or to scamper at hide-and-seek between the boles of the nearest pines.

To mark the day, 'the officers', King said, 'did me the pleasure of their company to dinner', prisoners were pardoned their local crimes, and there was a wholesale marrying and christening by the Rev. Mr. Johnson, who had come over to settle such matters retrospectively during the few days before the *Atlantic* sailed again for Sydney.[1]

Government House was a dilapidated little building twenty-four feet by twelve, falling to pieces and unsafe to live in. The Kings not only lived in it and had young Chapman to live there too, but their son was born there six weeks after their landing. They called him Phillip Parker, after their good friends the Governor and the Captain of the *Gorgon*.[2] On the day that the baby was born, Captain King found a store-keeper's job for William Chapman that took the young man to live at Phillipsburgh on the other side of the Island. One can imagine Mrs. King saying, 'My dear, you know I am very fond of William, but *really* . . .!' and thus a corner was found for the cradle. The dilapidated little house proving impossible, even without William, a grand new one, sixty feet long by thirty feet wide, was built by 'four very indifferent stonemasons' on a commanding situation behind the old one.

William walked across the Island daily to mess at the Governor's table, and there was much pleasant traffic between the Kings' house and his own.

'Mrs. King comes and spends a fortnight or three weeks at a time with me,' he wrote; 'she brings her little boy with her, or rather her young boy for he is the biggest child I ever saw of his age. It is a very pleasant walk from this place to the other side of the Island where the Governor lives, through a thick wood; I can compare it to nothing but some gentleman's park.'

The Governor, he said, behaved to him like a father, and Mrs. King treated him like a sister; and, when gout assailed the Governor, William became his right-hand man.

And King had need of a right-hand man, particularly one

[1] King's *Journal*.   [2] *Chapman Papers*.

NORFOLK ISLAND

of Chapman's sweet temper. Things had progressed in the seventeen months of King's absence—there were more people, more crops, more animals, and more houses; but there was also more ill feeling.

'After a week's pleasant passage', King wrote privately to Under-Secretary Nepean in London, 'I landed here on the 4th instant, when I found discord and strife on every person's countenance, and in every corner of the island, which you may easily conceive would render this an exact emblem of the infernal regions. I am pestered with complaints, bitter revilings, back-biting, and almost everything to begin over again.'

What had become of the Island Paradise? The gentleman's park-like prospect still pleased, but man was increasingly vile. The convicts were of a worse character than before, and many of them, after ill treatment on the voyage, were too debilitated to work, while others would rather starve than exert themselves; the few free settlers considered that nobody but they should have the right to grow stock or grain; the soldiers despised both convicts and free settlers, and thought themselves entitled to free rations even if every one else went short. Food was a problem, though not as acute a one as in Sydney because plentiful fish and seasonal flocks of mutton-birds helped to eke out supplies, and the soil was rich; but there were destructive pests to contend with and few of the people knew anything of agriculture. In the same way there was a general ignorance of the skilled trades and, as in Sydney, a distressing shortage of the most ordinary tools. Dysentery periodically afflicted the Island, hunger led to thieving and also rendered the thieves unfit to receive the several hundred lashes that were the punishment for the crime of stealing food.

Conceptions of mercy and justice have changed since then. In those days, officials accepted the lash and leg-irons without question as a necessary part of penal routine. Under King's rule, a woman on the Island was executed for robbery; captured runaways were sentenced to hard labour in chains for the rest of their term of transportation; a youth —'a hardened wretch' of eighteen years old—awaiting trial for repeated crimes was chained to the public grindstone until he could be sent to Port Jackson; while women convicted of blasphemous or indecent language had their hair shaved and were whipped at the cart's tail. Brutal as these measures are, by modern standards, there is plenty of evidence to show that King never became hardened to suffering in others and was by temperament less interested in punishment than in reform. When first he went to the Island, we are told that he drew round him the handful of people whose loneliness he shared, treating them 'with the kind attention which a good family meets with at the hands of a humane master'. When they turned out to be a bad family, planning to capture their guardian and escape to Otaheite, King became disillusioned but not unjust.[1] Again he was aware of the risks of giving to overseers the right to beat convicts, as so many of them 'would be perfect brutes if not restrained', and he stated publicly his intention to grant 'the rights of humanity' to convicts—that is, they were not to be insulted or attacked with impunity by free men.[2]

King, in fact, like Governor Phillip, really was a humane man. Within the limits of contemporary standards he was just, and he was as merciful as it was safe to be on that remote island. He had no greater powers than those of a justice of the peace, so that every serious crime had to be tried in Sydney—and every convict on the Island knew it.

[1] *Account of the English Colony in N.S.W.* i. 62.
[2] King's *Journal*.

In 1792 they were nine months without communication with Sydney, their only source of help and their only link with the outside world. News from England was often nine or twelve months old when it arrived, and the spasmodic postal arrangements were made even worse by the wars with revolutionary France. In 1794 King implored a friend 'to have the charity' to let him hear the news of Europe. On smaller matters connected with their own money affairs, in the casual hands of a London agent, they were often equally in the dark.

It was in this abnormal world that Mrs. King had to find personal happiness and bring up a family. Mrs. Paterson was her sole woman companion, and when the Patersons left after fifteen months no other officer's wife came to the Island until within a few months of the Kings' own departure. Two more children were born to them on the Island, two little girls, Maria in 1793 and Utricia in 1795. The infant Maria was usually facetiously referred to by young Chapman as 'my wife', the beautiful but delicate little Utricia, who did not live to grow up, was his god-daughter, and he called the boy Phillip his brother. Mrs King, who was so like Chapman that for years people took them for brother and sister, now became 'my mother-in-law' in his letters home. The friendly William was evidently very much one of the family.

For several months Mrs. King had to keep house for two curious guests of the Governor—two young Maoris, a warrior and a priest. Their visit was the result of a persistent official belief in the important trade that was expected from the New Zealand flax plant, found 'growing spontaneously' on Norfolk Island when Captain Cook discovered it in 1774. King had instructions to develop the industry, but all his attempts failed. 'I much fear', he wrote, 'that until a native

NORFOLK ISLAND

of New Zealand can be carried to Norfolk Island the method of dressing that valuable commodity will not be known; and could that be obtained, I have no doubt but Norfolk Island would very soon cloathe the inhabitants of New South Wales.'

When King wrote those words, he set the ball rolling that ultimately, by the round-about-the-globe methods of those leisurely days, brought him the Maori help that he wanted. He was in London at the time, and so was Captain George Vancouver, one of the able young officers who had sailed with Cook. King was soon to leave in the *Gorgon* for Norfolk Island, Vancouver in the *Discovery* for the north-west coasts of America. Vancouver's store-ship, the *Daedalus*, was to rendezvous with him in Nootka Sound, and was afterwards to go on to Port Jackson with livestock. Because of King's faith in the possibilities of flax, and the importance of taking any step that might reduce colonial costs to the mother-country, Vancouver was instructed that it was His Majesty's pleasure that the Captain of the *Daedalus* should 'touch at New Zealand and endeavour to take with him a flax-dresser or two, in order that the new settlers may, if possible, be instructed in the management of that valuable plant'. A little later, the ships *Gorgon* and *Discovery* met at the Cape, and there King personally pressed Vancouver, 'as an act of publick utility', to 'procure two natives of New Zealand'.

Everything went according to plan. Nearly two years later, the *Daedalus* anchored off a New Zealand beach. Two young Maoris, tempted by a desire for tools, went aboard, as they were intended to do. 'Blinded by the curious things they saw', they went below and while they were being entertained the *Daedalus* set sail. The Maoris wept, they tried to break the windows to get to their canoes, they filled the ship with lamentation; but His Majesty's pleasure had to be served and the *Daedalus* sailed on.[1]

When she anchored in Sydney Cove, a Calcutta ship was about to leave for India to fetch stock and grain for the Colony. Her captain had stores aboard for Norfolk Island: it was a simple matter to add the two Maoris to the goods to be delivered to Captain King.

With difficulty King explained to the Maoris the reason for their visit. At first they were sullen and uncommunicative, being apparently afraid that they would be made to work; but when at last they understood what was wanted of them, they taught all that they knew. After all that pother and heart-break, all that they knew was taught in an hour, as it turned out that flax-making was an occupation peculiar to the women. Alas for King's high hopes!

The question now was, what to do with the Maoris. They themselves had only one wish, to get home; but there was to be no chance of that for several months. King did his best; 'needless to say', he wrote, the Maoris slept at his house and ate at his table; and gradually they made friends. 'In their gloomy moments', says King, 'they threatened to commit suicide, but were laughed out of it.' The sight of Captain and Mrs. King, happy with their little Phillip and the infant Maria, must have made the two poor exiles all the more homesick; indeed, they were 'constantly lamenting their separation from their families and friends', and repeatedly begged King to send them home.[2]

By this time they had come to understand much of each other's language, and King had evidently grown very fond indeed of them. In fact, his interest in them and in the matter of flax, as well perhaps as an unacknowledged longing

[1] King's *Journal*, and his description appended to *The Account of the Colony of New South Wales*.   [2] King's *Journal*.

for a change such as even the most devoted of Governors and husbands must sometimes feel, led him to do something it is otherwise a little difficult to explain. When the *Britannia*, storeship, sailed for New Zealand with the Maoris on board, King, taking William Chapman and others, absented himself without head-quarters' leave and went too. For ten days, feeling assured every one would be good in his absence, he left that island prison in the charge of a visiting Captain of the New South Wales Corps.[1] As the sun sank each evening over the sea, bringing the Maoris one day nearer home, they chanted a sorrowful song about the separation from their wives and families, and King, listening in the fading light, found it 'very affecting'. When the ship anchored and King handed over his charges, there was a long dramatic song by their delighted friends describing all that had happened during their absence. There was a final exchange of gifts; there were warm farewells and no recriminations. The two Maoris 'cryed terribly', says Chapman, 'and everybody on board was much affected at the parting, particularly the Governor, who said he never parted with his mother with more regret than he did with those two men'.[2] The Maoris not only shed tears; they gave King two treasured greenstone *meres*, weapons imbued with the power of their owners' ancestors and not lightly bestowed.[3]

Nothing was ever to come of the flax venture, and King was strongly censured from Sydney for leaving his post; but, at least until he was made most unhappy by official disapproval, those ten days of beauty, pagan music, and romance must have been balm to his soul.

A little time after his return something happened that would seem to justify the disapproval of head-quarters.

[1] King's *Journal*.   [2] *Chapman Papers*.
[3] The *meres* are now exhibited at the Australian Museum, Sydney.

Some months earlier, Mr. William Balmain, assistant-surgeon and magistrate, had interested King in a proposal to allow some of 'the Free men and Convicts to get up a Play and to allow them to perform it on Saturdays, when they were perfect in their respective parts'. The idea appealed to King.

'As indulging them in this request did not interfere with the Publick work', says his journal, 'and as such amusement (when unattended with licentious behaviour) tend to unbend and divert the mind, I very readily gave my consent, and on condition that the Magistrate who made the application, would see it conducted with decency and propriety. With some little assistance, the scenery, &c. was well arranged and Two Plays were performed during this month, in which the Actors acquitted themselves with great propriety, and the utmost regularity and decency was observed.'

A month or so after King's return from New Zealand a play was to be performed on the anniversary of Queen Charlotte's birthday. The Kings and the officers who had dined with them were to attend. The story is best told in his own breathless words.

'Soon after I was seated', he writes, 'I observed several soldiers, with their hats on and very dirty sitting near and incommoding the Officers; after the Play was begun a soldier came into the House in a dirty check shirt without any Coat, and keeping his hat on (whilst I myself and every other Person was uncovered), placed himself in the most insolent Posture nearly opposite the seat I was sitting on; after he remained some time in that position, I desired one of the Officers of the Detachment who sat next to me, to order the soldier to take his hat off, which was done by the soldier with a peculiar insolence: as I was not then informed of a dispute which had taken place between a Constable and a Sergeant previous to my going into the House, I took no notice of the insolent behaviour of the soldier and the dirty appearance of his Comrades, wh. struck me most forcibly at this time, as I had always previous to this, observed that they were clean and orderly.

'The play was finished about ten o'clock, and soon after my return home, as I was walking on the Terrace opposite my house with Mr. Balmain (who was then informing me of the dispute, etc.) I heard a scuffle near the Play House and this Gentleman offered to see what occasioned it, but as I thought it was only some bustle occasioned by the People's crowding to get out of the Play House, I told him there was no necessity for it, as I thought they were dispersing, on which he left me and soon after he was gone I heard the noise increasing and Blows passing. I then ordered the Sergeant of the Guard to disperse the People, but finding that was not done so readily as I wished, and as it might have been done, and hearing a Man I distinctly saw, exclaiming with the most horrid Execrations "Put every man to death", at which time the Granary keeper came to me and begged me to interfere or Murder would ensue, and observing a Number of men run along the front paling of my House from the Barracks towards the place where the fray was with weapons of some kind in their hands (and which I afterwards found was the greatest part of the Detachment with their Bayonets) I found it necessary to interpose (not having any Person of Authority near me) I immediately went to the place wh. was only Fifteen yards from the spot where I was standing, and seized the above man (who was still uttering the most horrid Execrations and Threats) by the Shoulder, and without quitting my hold I delivered him to the Sergeant of the Guard.'

King then found that the man was George Bannister, the insolent soldier in the dirty check shirt.

It was, in fact, a very ugly incident, and must have been an alarming one for Mrs. King to listen to from inside the house after returning from the play. Next day the arms of the Detachment were secured by a stratagem and the Governor held an inquiry. He found that before his arrival at the play there had been an argument as to the division of seats between Mrs. King's servants and the soldiers, and blows had been struck; that what appeared to be a petty dispute was really a disturbance planned beforehand by the soldiers, who considered that the convicts were habitually favoured by Governor King. There was a plan to murder one convict whose wife a soldier had seduced, and a general mutiny was part of the plot.

The worst of the mutineers—twenty in number—were secured at Government House. The rest, much ashamed of themselves, admitted to being misled and had their arms returned after taking the oath of allegiance in front of the assembled inhabitants. A temporary militia guard was formed and order and confidence were restored.[1] By a chance schooner, the mutineers were sent for court martial to Sydney where King's conduct of this affair was as much disapproved as his going to New Zealand. In neither case was it Governor Phillip who censured him—he had returned to England, worn out at last; it was the Acting-Governor, Major Francis Grose, Commanding Officer of the New South Wales Corps, the man who stored up so much trouble for the Colony by transferring the power from civil to military hands as soon as Phillip's back was turned. In connexion with the disturbance on the Island, Grose stated that 'No provocation that a soldier can give is ever to be admitted as an excuse for a convict's striking a soldier'. It was just one shot in the battle for military ascendancy that played such a big part in the early history of New South Wales. Fortunately, Grose's harsh opinion of King's conduct was not shared by the Secretary of State, and Grose himself, when his temper cooled, took a milder view of the supposed affronts to himself and his Corps.

[1] King's *Journal*.

Throughout their régime in Norfolk Island, both the Kings seem to have been frequently ill, and indeed Mrs. King must have spent much of her time nursing her husband through attacks of gout. It is worth noting that before leaving England King left with his agent an order for an annual shipment of thirty-six dozen of port.[1] The available medical skill cannot have been high even according to contemporary lights. Amongst the assistant surgeons who served on the Island from time to time was a convict 'bred to surgery' who acquitted himself well, and D'Arcy Wentworth, whose famous son was born on the Island while the Kings were there. Wentworth, a lively young man with influential connexions, had come out as a free settler in the ill-famed Second Fleet, electing to do this on his acquittal at the Old Bailey on a charge of highway robbery.[2]

In 1793 two things happened that should have helped with the Governor's health—there was a plentiful supply of fresh meat grown on the Island, and King told his agent not to send any more port. In 1795, however, the Governor was so seriously ill that he was 'given up'. Had he died, Chapman was to have conveyed his widow and family, and his papers, to England. It was not long after the birth of the second and delicate little daughter: 'Mrs. King', says Chapman, 'has had a dreadful time of it'.

Next year King told Banks that after a long illness he was taking the advice of all his friends and applying for leave to return to England for proper medical advice. 'My Principal and most alarming complaint', he wrote, 'is an almost fixed compression of the Lungs and Breast, with a difficulty of Breathing and a constant Pain in the Stomach.' The expense of transporting his family was worrying him a good deal;

[1] *King Papers.*
[2] *Historical Record of Australia*, Series I, vol. i, note 290.

NORFOLK ISLAND

his salary, apart from his half-pay as a naval commander, was £250 a year, which he supplemented from the proceeds from thirty acres leased on the Island. On his way out, he had avowed his intention of keeping his hands and heart as clean as his friend Phillip's, and this he did. To Banks he said, 'As I have neither kept a shop or sold drams, my worldly savings do not exceed £1,000—so I shall not return a Nabob'.[1] This last was a hit at the unscrupulous trade monopoly established in Sydney by officers of the New South Wales Corps.

In April, 1796, King and his family sailed in the storeship *Britannia*. Chapman found the parting with the Governor and his dear Mrs. King 'very afflicting'. 'I have one consolation', he told his mother, 'that keeps up my spirits, which is that he returns to Europe for his own advantage Health and Interest, till I hear from him I shall live in hopes of seeing him once more in the Colony. . . .'

His hope was to be fulfilled.

The voyage in the *Britannia*, 300 tons, with little Phillip, Maria, and the fourteen months old Utricia, was made to the Cape in three months, and there they trans-shipped to the East-Indiaman *Contractor*.[2] On board this ship their third daughter, Elizabeth, was born. Years afterwards Mrs. King wrote words of heart-felt gratitude for the kindness she had received from the *Contractor's* Captain and the mate.[3] The complications of that voyage must have made the journey to Sydney in H.M.S. *Gorgon* seem to the Kings in retrospect a comfortable pleasure cruise.

[1] *Banks Papers*, vol. 18.
[2] King preceded them to England, in the *Marquis Cornwallis*. See Appendix I.
[3] *Piper Papers*, p. 369.

CHAPTER III

Standing by

1797–1799

THE Kings arrived in England in May 1797. At first they presumably spent much of their time in looking for the health, never to be his, that King had come home to find; but soon there was something else he sought, and that was work.

King had no certainty of further employment by the Home Department and, it seemed, owing to the length of his civilian period, no prospect of renewed service with the Navy. Being idle did not suit his energetic nature or the state of his purse, and in his anxiety the inevitable man to turn to was Sir Joseph Banks. Ever since the days when, as a young 'gentleman of large fortune well versed in natural history', Banks and his suite of eight had accompanied Captain Cook in the *Endeavour*, he had maintained his interest in New Holland, and now he was patron-saint of the colony that he had helped to found. In all its affairs, political and scientific, he was the power behind the throne. In the face of general opinion he believed in the future of the settlement and kept official interest in it alive in spite of ministerial preoccupation with war and revolution. He declined to align himself with either side in politics—refused, indeed, to be a Minister of the Crown in order the better to be a friend to the colony, describing himself as a bird of peace, and his particular business as that of an encourager of the transport of plants from one country to another. It was a modest claim for one of international standing in science. Little ships crossing the seas between

STANDING BY

England and Rio de Janeiro, England and Russia, the Indies, and the Cape of Good Hope, carried new specimens for the President of the Royal Society, the great Sir Joseph Banks, or boxes of plants sent by him from Kew Garden for acclimatization in distant parts of the world. The carrying of bread-fruit trees from Otaheite to the West Indies was Sir Joseph's plan, and before the *Bounty* sailed on her ill-starred voyage Bligh wrote to him 'Difficulties I laugh at whilst I have your countenance'. So it was with successive governors of New South Wales: whatever their troubles, while they had his countenance all was not lost.

After some months of waiting on Whitehall doorsteps, varied by visits to his wife and family in the West, King unburdened himself to Banks. He was hurt that the Admiralty seemed now to look upon him as an alien; he seriously thought of resigning the dormant commission of Lieutenant-Governor of New South Wales obtained for him earlier by Banks. 'If I can get employed . . . it will be well', he wrote; 'if not, I must go into Wales or Cornwall, and take up my spade.' Devoted civil service, it seemed, even in those days of naval activity, could leave a sailor high and dry.

Employment came at last. Phillip had long ago recommended King as the best man to succeed himself as Governor of New South Wales; another naval officer, Captain Hunter, had applied for the post and been appointed instead: now, thanks partly to the influence of Banks, Hunter was to be succeeded by King.

One wonders what Mrs. King's feelings were at this stage; very much, one imagines, what a woman's are now when the husband to whose interests she is devoted is given a responsible post in a place where the children she loves cannot go—a mixture of gratification and sorrow, of anxiety and pride. The fragile Utricia was now dead; the little

Elizabeth born at sea was to go to sea with them again, but Phillip and Maria, aged eight and six, were to be left behind. The good-byes were not to be said for a long time, but the Kings did not know that.

Some time before his appointment, King had seen an advertisement in the papers for two ships for the use of the Colony in New South Wales. Being in London and thinking that his knowledge of colonial transport needs might be of use, he called at the office of the Navy Board to offer his help. It was accepted, and with Sir John Henslow, Chief Surveyor of the Navy, he inspected a number of ships and chose the only one suitable in height and tonnage, the *Buffalo*. For a long time King heard no more of the business; then, learning indirectly that a second ship was being especially built for the Board and that she was of faulty design, he went down to the yards and took a look for himself. One look, apparently, was enough. She was 'so extremely short, deep and full' that he commented on it to the builder and overseer. He found them of the same opinion as himself; the three stood there beside the frame and agreed that if she were not changed she would turn out 'a very bad ship'. Would Captain King speak to Sir John Henslow about it and ask for her to be lengthened ten or twelve feet?—it could be easily done, said the builder. Two days later, at the launching of a warship, King got his opportunity and mentioned his apprehensions to Sir John: but Sir John 'thought she would turn out a very good ship, and that she was too far advanced to lengthen'.

In May 1798, when King had been a year in England, he got his sailing orders, and the vessel that was chosen to carry him and his family across the world was the very ship of his apprehensions. She was now launched and soon to be out of her uneasy builder's hands and was known as

His Majesty's armed ship *Porpoise*. The baggage was put on board, and from then on the Kings had to hold themselves in readiness to embark.

It did not at that time seem that there was to be much delay. The optimistic Henslow had gone to much trouble over the accommodation of the various passengers, and by June the only thing awaiting decision was the construction of a deck-shelter for the plants 'usefull in food or physic' that the *Porpoise* was to carry out for the colony. A plant-cabin, it was called, a structure six feet by twelve designed by Sir Joseph Banks. Deck superstructures must have been a tender subject with Sir Joseph; years before, the removal of the one erected for him on board Cook's *Resolution* had resulted in his withdrawal from the second expedition and a temporary coolness between him and Cook. This time, when applied to by the Navy Board for his advice, Banks walked warily. Was the Board sure that the size he recommended to hold the plant boxes would not be too large and cause inconvenience in working the ship? He was assured that all was well.

So the plant-cabin was built, the plants brought at intervals from Kew, and a botanist and two gardeners came aboard to take care of them on the voyage. There were vines, hops, apples, pears, peaches, nectarines, nuts, and herbs; and there were more delicate things such as ginger, cactus, camphor, and strawberries. There was very little room for them, and they 'disputed the quarter-deck' with the *Porpoise's* brass guns; in addition, King hung six seed-baskets in his own cabin, where he hoped the fire that he would be obliged to have would do the seeds no harm.

Time was getting on. The summer was long past, autumn gone, and Christmas upon them before the ship left the Thames at last on her way round to Portsmouth where she was to pick up the Kings. And before she left Margate Roads all King's apprehensions proved to be justified. They had to put back to Sheerness with the loss of two anchors and after ample proof that the vessel was unmanageable. Between the Nore and Margate the master 'had the mortification' to see several small vessels pass him with all their small sails set while he dare not put even a moderate amount of sail on the *Porpoise*; from Sheerness to Portsmouth, when after further delay she sailed again, he was embarrassed at being scarcely able to keep ahead of the eighty-two merchant vessels to whom she was supposed to be acting as convoy, and at the Downs the pilot refused to take charge of the ship. In fact, she was 'so very crank as to be scarce sea-worthy'.

The fault, said the master, was her great top-weight; the remedy he proposed was the removal of the plant-cabin from the quarter-deck and the stowing of the boxes between decks. King held different views. He lamented risking the loss to the Colony of 'so rich a treasure' as the plant collection by putting it away from the air and suggested instead the removal of the high barricaded quarters aft and the lengthening of the *Porpoise's* keel. He never had had any opinion of the ship as a sailer—she was 'certainly the worst calculated' he had ever seen. The Masters of the West Indiamen under her convoy had had some very unflattering things to say of her sailing and steering in the Channel: in the dangerous seas to which she was going there was great risk of her being pooped. But even supposing her to arrive safely at Port Jackson, she was, as King pointed out to the Board, unlikely to survive the conditions she would meet in the colonial service, carrying goods to Norfolk Island and bringing cattle from the Cape.

It was a grim prospect. Yet even now it was only

reluctantly that the Navy Board decided to make the alterations to rudder and keel, their natural inclination being to blame the high position of Banks's 'little conservatory of plants' rather than the shortcomings of their own hit-and-miss theories of naval design. The *Porpoise*, with all her stores and baggage still aboard, went into dock; and the facetious Portsmouth critics who saw her there said that the rudder had been placed at the wrong end of the ship.

All this delay was disastrous to the finances of the Kings. When the *Porpoise* first left the river, lodgings in Blackheath were exchanged for lodgings in Portsmouth at war prices. As the months dragged by, their small savings vanished and finally King began to spend in advance the salary that he would not begin to receive until he took up his duties in New South Wales. Added to this, all the perishable stores put on board months earlier were ruined by the damp of the ship and had to be replaced. To his great regret, he decided that he could not now afford to leave Phillip to be educated in England but must take him to New South Wales. To Banks he wrote, 'I beg most sincerely for a term to be put to our anxious situation. I really look back with no [small] degree of temper at the time I have been in a state of almost daily expectation of sailing—now eight months!!! . . .'

When the *Porpoise* left Portsmouth Dockyard the impoverished King and his wife, with Phillip and Elizabeth, went to live on board. Humbler passengers had been living in the ship for months, amongst them the two gardeners and the wife of one of them, with a new-born baby, and George Caley, the semi-educated young botanist going to the colony at the expense of Banks. It was crowded, uncomfortable, and none too clean: but King was four

STANDING BY

hundred pounds in debt and the disagreeable accommodation was free.

At last the ship was ready to sail, but now the rumoured activity of the French Fleet kept her in harbour still; and when the French were said to be gone and convoys left for the East and West Indies and for Lisbon, no sailing orders came for the *Porpoise* to go with them. 'I fear we are forgot at the Admiralty', said the exasperated King. 'Every now and then great bustle is made', wrote Caley, 'and we are going to sea immediately'; but they never did. At last Caley, to avoid a verminous neighbour and relieve his feelings, walked to London and back, while King, debts notwithstanding, took Mrs. King and the children ashore again, this time to the Isle of Wight.

The only imperturbable passengers were the precious plants. Through the changing seasons of 1798 and 1799, in the Thames, the Channel, or at Portsmouth, the vines and hops stayed healthy, and the mulberries, filberts and quinces, the willows and the oaks, flourished among the hammering of carpenters and the confusion of an overcrowded ship. King looked forward hopefully to the day when he could report to Banks that the whole collection was through the tropics and the wintry southern seas and safe landed in New South Wales.

In September, the last good-byes were said and the *Porpoise* set sail. With a fleet of two hundred other ships she was carried out of the Channel into the Bay. There was a favourable wind and a mild sea; she still steered indifferently but seemed improved by the changes made; King was almost reconciled and Mrs. King, busying herself with unpacking, must have begun to feel at ease. And then all their hopes were shattered. With no bad weather to try her, her tiller carried away and her rudder was dangerously sprung. It blew a gale, and she lay to until they could communicate with the Admiral of the Convoy, when she was at once ordered back to the first English port.

King's letter to Banks, written after their return to Spithead, is surprisingly restrained. He did, however, permit himself to say that the *Porpoise* was better fitted for a canal than for the open sea; and to the Navy Board, uninvited, he repeated his old opinion that she was too short and would never do. At this moment of acute disappointment and a return to the worries of life ashore, it cannot have helped to hear that the gossips were saying that the *Porpoise* had been built to his plan.

This time there could be no question of tinkering with the ship. By the Navy Board, King said, he was not viewed *de bon œil*; but the Admiralty was different: they sought his opinion, and as a result of his frank report the *Porpoise* was at once condemned. At his suggestion she was replaced by a copper-bottomed Spanish prize then lying at Portsmouth almost ready for sea. The stores, the plants, and the passengers were to be transferred to the new *Porpoise*, together with the spars and rigging, the officers and crew of the old. But the Kings were to wait no longer. They were to sail almost at once in the whaler *Speedy*, and the botanist Caley, to his joy, was to go with them in the Governor's suite. In the meantime the young man was relieving his feelings once more by walking *via* Salisbury to London and back.

And the plants of which the Colony was so badly in need? At the end of 1799 King told Banks that no hothouses in England could produce plants in as fine order as those in the garden on board. A year later, when the substitute *Porpoise* reached Sydney, every one of them was dead.

CHAPTER IV

Return to Sydney

1799–1800

BEFORE sailing in the *Speedy*, the Kings had one rearrangement to make. Some measure of compensation had been promised to King for the expenses of the delay, so after all Phillip was to be put to school in England. In a few years he was to enter the Navy; to condemn him in the meantime to a haphazard colonial education—to be tutored by an emancipated gentleman convict or by some unlettered clerk—was a risk that they were not prepared to run. They suffered their parental pangs and left him behind. Maria was safe at Greenwich with friends; Phillip was now handed over to the Rev. Peter Thomas Burford of the Academy, Stratford Grove, within the orbit of the penny post and a twice daily coach from the Saracen's Head. There he was to receive board and education in Greek, Latin, French, and English, writing and Accompts for the annual sum of £26. 5s.[1]

There is pathos in the letter to the schoolmaster so carefully written in the third person by King, in which he says that Phillip's parents

'leave him with the utmost confidence in the protection he will receive from Mr. and Mrs. Burford and they do not doubt but that the great distance they will be removed from their child, his extreme youth, and having never been from his mother, will be sufficient claims on the peculiar attention of Mr. Burford and the female part of the family'.

There was a list of the people with whom the boy might stay in the holidays, and he was not to stay more than one

[1] *King Papers.*

week with any one, and not to get more than three pence a week pocket money; and they wished Mr. Burford to let them have news of him *twice a year*. There were guardians appointed—in Maria's case not less than four including Governor King's mother and his agent Mr. James Sykes: but in the case of Maria—'our Darling Girl'—of education there was not one word.[1]

At last in November 1799 they sailed from Spithead in the whaler *Speedy*. She carried fifty women convicts and stores for the colony and was one of a large fleet under the convoy of two ships of war. It was not long since Nelson's victory at the Nile, but, Nelson notwithstanding, as far as Mrs. King was concerned the shadow of Napoleon lay darkly over the first few weeks of the voyage. In her diary[2] she writes that she fears nothing but capture. In a spell of calm weather she exclaims, 'Such days as these would be called pleasant, but I confess *coward as I am*, I should rather prefer a breeze provided the wind is fair...'

From the first, King's health dominates the diary. After a time, fear of capture by the French Fleet was left behind, but never does Mrs. King lose her dread of that enemy, the gout. Two days after sailing, her husband was seized with a violent cold and rheumatism, which Mrs. King attributes to damp beds improperly aired in the hurry of their departure, and for a fortnight he was 'ill with gout in every part'. Three weeks later—certainly after a Christmas dinner of 'a Boiled Leg of Mutton, three Roast Fowls, a very fine Ham with as good a Mince Pye as could be made on board ship'—she records, 'King very Ill Gout flying about him'; two days later he is still 'dangerously ill'. By March he is mending, and fortunately during a bad gale in the 'roaring

---

[1] Arrangements had also been made for the care and education of Norfolk and Sydney. See Appendix I.   [2] Mitchell Library MSS.

forties' he was quite well: had he been laid up, Mrs. King knows not what they would have done.

There is one thing that he finds very comforting, and that is his warm bath, a form of treatment apparently unusual enough to merit description. 'It is a large Tin Shoe, painted Green, big enough to put his whole body into, when he bathes it is placed under the companion outside the cabin door when it is filled with warm water a sail is thrown over the companion which covers him from everything'. He 'enjoys it twice a week and finds it does him much service. I often take a dip after him'. When the *Speedy* anchors in Table Bay it is most inexplicably known at once that Captain King is on board the whaler—from another ship a naval officer with a sharp eye has spied the tin bath and spread the news. 'When we heard of our Signal', says Mrs. King, 'it caused some little mirth.'

The tropics cause prickly heat and general sickliness and some of the passengers are seriously ill, including little Elizabeth. Near Trinidad—a small uninhabited island in the Atlantic, near the Tropic of Capricorn—a woman named Butler goes out of her mind and dies, and some days later there was 'a great outcry amongst the Ladies', as Mrs. King calls the convict women, that they had seen her spirit amongst them in the night. Another woman dies, leaving an orphan infant whose care gives Mrs. King much concern. A child dies, and others of the women, and after Cape Town the doctor becomes insane. Fortunately the busy Mrs. King remains more or less well throughout, though a prey to nervous fears; and these perhaps she confides mostly to her diary.

Heat and any rough weather make conditions uncomfortable, and Mrs. King feels a very deep pity for the convict women, 'often battened down and for all this precaution they and their bedding getting as wet as drowned rats'.

RETURN TO SYDNEY

In spite of this when they are used to it they seem all very merry and happy, 'and indeed cannot be otherwise when every indulgence is properly allowed to them'. On Xmas Day they had a little dance for about two hours, the Governor's party looking on with much amusement. 'Some attempted Irish and some Scotch steps and in truth I could scarcely make out any sort of steps but a Country Jump.' On another day,

'This being Sunday, our Ladies dressed out very neat and clean excepting one that calls herself Lady Underhill—she complains very much that she cannot bear the things Government has provided for her, and unfortunately she has but very few others. I never saw such a proud creature in all my life, and with all her rags and dirt would you believe that she mounts a muslin Turban which is oftener as black as Ink than it is white, then when her Ladyship employs a person to wash it—she wears a black ribbon.'

There is a suggestion of the up-turned nose in this anecdote: in the following entry the disapproval is of a deeper sort.

'The Captain', she writes, 'had reason to punnish one of the Boys for a Guilt occasioned by a woman of the name of Ward—for which she was also to be punished by being pumped on (the only punishment the Captain has ever inflicted on any of them) this woman has often been heard to say that if ever she was pumped on that she would Jump over-board the next moment—and sure enough she did—and was it not for the very great Expeditious manner with which the Captain ordered the boat down took in sail (and at this time we was going seven knots) she must have been lost her clothes kept her up as long as she did, and when the boat got to her she was sinking—but the mate was very quick in his motions and got her up—it Pleased god that she should not be drowned. She was fortunately placed into the Boat with her head hanging downwards—(and this was mear chance) the water of course ran out of her mouth, nose and Ears—when she was brought alongside the ship she was hoisted up in the boat—and when she was taken into the ship I really thought she was dead, the Doctor used every means for her recovery, one of which I shall observe—he gave her three Teaspoonfuls of Ground Pepper in a Glass of Red wine—a most powerful medicine but wonderful quick in the Effect for Immediately as it was put down her throat the salt water came off her stomach—three Emetticks. She is recovering. It has given me such a turn against them her conduct, as well as all the rest, that I shall be happy to get to the end of our voyage, as soon as possible.'

Animals play a part in the diary. A pair of ducks find their way from betwixt decks into the Kings' quarters; a goose falls through an open skylight on to the company at dinner below, overturning Mrs. King's glass of porter just as she was 'going to Drink the Delicious Draught' and causing 'a good laugh'; their largest hog tumbles down the main hatchway and breaks some ribs—most unfortunate, because they have just killed a sheep. When they get into the cold southerly seas 'the stock do but very indifferent, sheep and fowls dying fast.'

It is not only the animals that suffer falls. Jane Dundas, formerly Governor Phillip's housemaid[1] and now Mrs. King's, tumbles down the companion stairs and bruises herself so badly that she scarcely can move, nor can she lie in bed, and every time the ship lurches she is ready to scream out with pain. A boy falls and nearly bites off his tongue; Elizabeth falls and every one thinks she is killed; a convict woman pitches down the main hatchway and splinters her leg very badly and another scalds her foot—'In fact, the ship rolls and tumbels about so much that I wonder how the Sailors keeps on their Legs. For my part on those days I with Elizabeth keeps close to our state room lest any accident should happen to her.'

[1] *Pioneers of Sydney Cove.*

RETURN TO SYDNEY

One day, the ship's lurch had fatal consequences. The Kings, the Captain, and Second Mate had just finished dinner when there was an outcry on deck that a man was overboard. To Mrs. King's great concern it turned out to be Mr. Wise, the master-weaver, who was going out to take charge of the Government manufacture of linen and wool. He had been out in the mizzen chains and 'returning he had got both legs over the Side of the Ship when the mizzen sheet struck him—he let go his hold and down he went, into the water. Immediate assistance was given, boat down, and was looking for him—and nothing was seen but his hat.' The weaver's instant disappearance was ascribed by Mrs. King and other onlookers to a combination of heavy clothing and timid nature. He left a very young wife and two children to continue a miserable voyage without him, and Mrs. King was much distressed on their behalf. His death was going to prove a serious loss to the colony.

Another man was luckier, or perhaps possessed of more courage, than Mr. Wise the Weaver. He fell overboard while helping with repairs after a storm and it was half an hour before they could reach him in one of the boats. All this time he

'kept himself up notwithstanding we had a very heavy Swell—and which hurt him very much—however the boat got to him just in time and I am happy to say he was saved—he said that he could not have held it out much longer, for that he found himself going—he kicked off his shoes he said, a bird kept close before him all the time he was in the water—he also called to the ship every moment, and the people answering him—poor fellow, he surprised me very much to see him walk when he came on board—he was taken care of, put to bed, and made comfortable'.

One fine day with a fair breeze their log showed 225 miles. 'I never', says Mrs. King, 'remember to have gone such a number of miles in my whole life in one day.' ... 'We are spinning a fine long thread towards the Cape of Good Hope.' And all the time she was getting farther and farther away from the children in England. They drank Phillip's health on his birthday and thought especially of him on the day that he was to begin his holidays, as he would be missing his parents all the more. 'As to dear Maria, I feel very easy on her account; she is under the protection of a Worthy and Sincere Friend who is more like a Mother to her than anything else.'

Ten days at the Cape were a very welcome break after more than ten weeks at sea, although the voyage so far was described by King as 'pleasant and expeditious'. Since the *Gorgon's* visit, the Colony had changed hands and the British were now in possession.[1] As before, there was much hospitality, both English and Dutch.

'Our mornings,' says Mrs. King, 'were much taken up by receiving and paying visits, Invitations pouring in hourly for dinnerparties which filled up the whole of the time of our stay. I received very great attention from all the English, and indeed I should not do Justice to the Dutch if I did not allow them to be very civil, but it was from another *motive* that their *civilities* was so *spontaneous*'.

She was much struck with the charm and good manners of the bride of General Dundas, the Commander-in-Chief, having known her as plain Miss Cuming at the Isle of Wight and finding her not at all puffed up now that she was the first lady in rank.[2]

[1] In 1803 the Colony was handed back to the Batavian Republic (Holland) under the terms of the Peace of Amiens. During renewed hostilities it was captured by the British in 1806 and has remained under British rule since that date.
[2] The Governor, Sir George Young, had not brought his wife to Capetown.

It may have been the overwhelming amount of hospitality that made Mrs. King omit to mention another of their hostesses—the lovely Lady Anne Barnard, wife of the Governor's Secretary and the then unacknowledged author of the famous ballad, 'Auld Robin Gray'. In the sparkling pages of the Lady Anne's letters to her friend the great Lord Melville, Secretary of State for Scotland, Cape Town, with its feuds and flirtations, its big problems and little intrigues, comes to life. Everything interested and amused her; she entertained everybody.

'We had a Botany Bay Captain dining with us t'other day',[1] she wrote: 'I beg its pardon, by the bye, for I find Botany Bay takes it ill to be so called; New South Wales is its name. He is carrying a freight of bullocks from Cape Town—about 200.... The Captain of the ship gave me a very pleasing account of Botany Bay (I beg its pardon again) and the reformation it works on individuals, most of whom become honest members of the community.'

Soon afterwards the Kings were at her house—

'good people, I think, and apparently well-suited to their destination.... I sent a present of a silk gown to a rogue there, transported by Margaret [her sister] and me; the only creature I believe we ever punished or prosecuted in our lives. But she was too great a thief to let pass. If she is reformed (and that is easily found out) Mrs. King is to give her a few encouraging lines from me, and the gown; if she continues bad, I have begged her to give it as a wedding-gown to the first young girl of good Botany Bay character who is married after her arrival.'[2]

The Kings were about to embark when they were pressed by the frivolous old Governor, Sir George Young, and other

[1] Captain Kent, Governor Hunter's nephew, of H.M.S. *Buffalo*, who brought the first merino rams to New South Wales.
[2] *South Africa a Century Ago*, by W. H. Wilkins, pp. 276-8.

friends to stay one day longer so that they might go to the Assembly. King was anxious to get on with the voyage, but his wife had brought ashore a festive frock and wanted to wear it. 'With much reluctance I must say King consented that we should stay.'

'Expecting an amusement of this kind,' says Mrs. King, 'I had provided myself with a dress, so that I was not only ready in mind and wish, but dress also—therefore I had nothing to think of but to recollect my Scotch steps in which, by the bye, I believe I gave my master some credit. The Assembly Room is not so long as the Blackheath Assembly room, nor near so wide. We danced in Two Sets, about fifty couples in each set, we English ladies felt ourselves much crowded and pushed about by the Dutch, who are very fond of throwing about their Legs and at a Strange rate. Mrs. Dundas led off the first dance, I stood next to her, a Mrs. Smith and a Mrs. Crawford with us were the only English ladies in that set—when I got to the bottom of the room one of the Dutch ladies said to me—"you must sit down now you have got to the bottom of the room, you see how many couple you have not danced down, and they will never dance if you don't sit down". We therefore took ourselves to the other end of the room and sat ourselves down—had I been in England I should have thought I had behaved extremely rude, by attempting to sit down before the dance was quite finished. In fact the Cape ladies are the most impolite set I ever met with in all my life, *if possible* they are ten times worse than ever—at half past Eleven o'clock the Supper was announced, and such a squeeze I never shall forget, it put me in mind of going to the Pit at some of our charming Playhouses and at some particular benefit—my poor gold muslin had nearly been torn to pieces . . . we had a very good supper, at least at the part of the table I was at. Dancing after supper was well attended by the Dutch Frows and young "bucks" who I find kept it up till morning. We quiet people departed in peace after supper, for my part I had more on my mind than Sleep, as we was to Embark in the morning—the Captain Expecting to sail as soon as we was on board.'

They were coming to the worst part of the voyage and the Captain was as anxious as King to have it behind him.

Soon after sailing, Mrs. King's sensibilities were shocked at the sight of 'five large whales, which gave such a howl and a Jump, at the same time, out of the water' that she 'was very much terrified at such an alarm'. It was a very fine evening and night, but she dreads bad weather 'on the whales account'.

And bad weather, inevitably, they have. While still near the land a gale splits their mizzen mast, and Mrs. King is terrified at learning that the ship is making a great deal of water—indeed, she can hear it washing in under the counter and it comes in from one end of the ship to the other. Masculine reassurances must have been offered, for in the next entry she says that she understands that the leak is above water and that water comes in 'only when the ship dips'. She pulls herself together and praises the carefulness of the Captain, the behaviour of the ship, and the attention of the whole ship's company. The mast is mended and she is told that it is now stronger than when new; doubtfully, she hopes it will last out the voyage.

This is the moment that the doctor chooses to become definitely unhinged. At the Cape the medical man had pronounced him mad, and shaved and blistered his head, and now, says Mrs. King, already in a tremor at night with listening for water leaking in, now 'he *looks mad* and *acts mad*, he gets up in the middle of the night, comes down into the cabin—frightens us out of our wits ... God knows what his disorder can have been, but curious it is that the woman named Butler was just in the same way—only that she really died and he only talked about it.' She longs for moderate weather so that the leak can be mended—though the Captain tells her it is of no consequence—but even the idea of a leak on board is, she says, enough for her, she has grown such a coward.

Worse was to come. At the end of March they were nearing the South Cape of New Holland[1]—too near for their comfort in such cloudy weather—and there was threat in the sky. At noon the wind began to blow, and increased so that

'at half past one this morning it blew so heavy that the Captain took in all sail but such as was necessary to keep the ship steady—and brought her too—the sea was dreadful, which with the wind kept on encreasing—at half past four o'clock a Sea Struck and made a breach over the Larboard side of the ship carrying away all before it. It stripped the Starboard side of the Railing, and Hanchings, and the Boat cranes—all three water casks that was only put there the day before of course all went—(and the poor Bathing Shoe)—everybody's cabin suffered by this dreadful sea. It burst down upon me, and poor Elizabeth, and compleatly wetted us through bed and all, and the bottom part of the Cabin was shoe-deep with water—for my part I thought the decks were falling in upon us and that we was in great danger, the very great crash that was on deck made me conjecture everything to be going—Captain calling out cut away—overboard—cut away—overboard—it shocked me very much—in a few minutes King brought me word that we was not in the least danger—Daylight coming on fast I flattered myself that it would moderate a little—but to the contrary.'

For three hours it continued to blow

'so dreadful that to Speak my real thoughts I expected every

[1] The definite existence of a strait between the mainland of Australia and Van Diemen's Land, suspected since Bass's whale-boat voyage in 1797, and proved by Bass and Flinders in 1798-9, was not known in England until after the *Speedy* sailed. Her captain might have heard of it at the Cape, but in any case he would have preferred the known risks of the passage by the South Cape to the dangers of the uncharted strait. The *Lady Nelson*, 60 tons, Lieut. Grant, was the first ship from England to sail through the Strait, arriving in Sydney in December 1800.

moment that we should be lost. .... At 12 o'clock it began to abate a little.... By four o'clock we could visibly see it moderate, and thank God we are once more preserved from the raging seas.'

One fright they had was of a different sort. One Sunday the Captain on deck and the Kings in their cabin were alarmed at the same moment by a great smoke and a smell.

'In the morning the Captain's servant had been down in the gunroom under our Cabin to get at a box for King, and he had left the candle burning in this place for more than one hour, when the candle burnt down to its end, it caught the bag he had fastened it to by the sticking of the grease to the bag—which was rice belonging to us—this was smouldering away and at last got to another bag of Twine—when the smell was more distinct of fire, and the smoke all together alarmed us just in good time— had it gone further God only knows what our lots would have been for the Gun room is as full as possible of everything that would have burnt at a great rate and a cask or Two of Spirits would have helped to have blown us up. I ran upon Deck and at that time it was raining as hard as it well could, in fact I did not know where to go, for all I thought was over—we must be lost. ... It cannot be supposed but that these little frights makes me something of a coward, for *this* is my *name* now, and I cannot help it, nor shall I try to get it removed as I trust, please God I live, my next voyage will be my last—When I am going that, the thoughts that I shall have will keep up my Spirits, and I shall not care what weather we shall have, provided the wind is fair—because the faster we go the sooner I shall be blest with the sight of my dearest Children—may god Grant, that we may all live to return.'

They arrived at Port Jackson in April 1800, having been five months at sea.

SYDNEY IN 1788
From a sketch by Captain Hunter

SYDNEY IN 1798

VUE DE LA PARTIE MÉRIDIONALE DE LA VILLE DE SYDNEY

From a drawing by Lesueur, of the Baudin Expedition, 1803

This was Mrs. King's view

VUE D'UNE PARTIE DE LA VILLE DE SYDNEY

Showing Government House, with the veranda, and, to the right of the masts, the roof of the Orphanage

From a drawing by Lesueur, of the Baudin Expedition, 1803

GOVERNOR KING

Miniature: artist and date unknown
By permission of the Trustees of the Mitchell Library, Sydney

WILLIAM CHAPMAN
Ring miniature; artist and date unknown
In the possession of the Misses Chapman, Frankston, Victoria

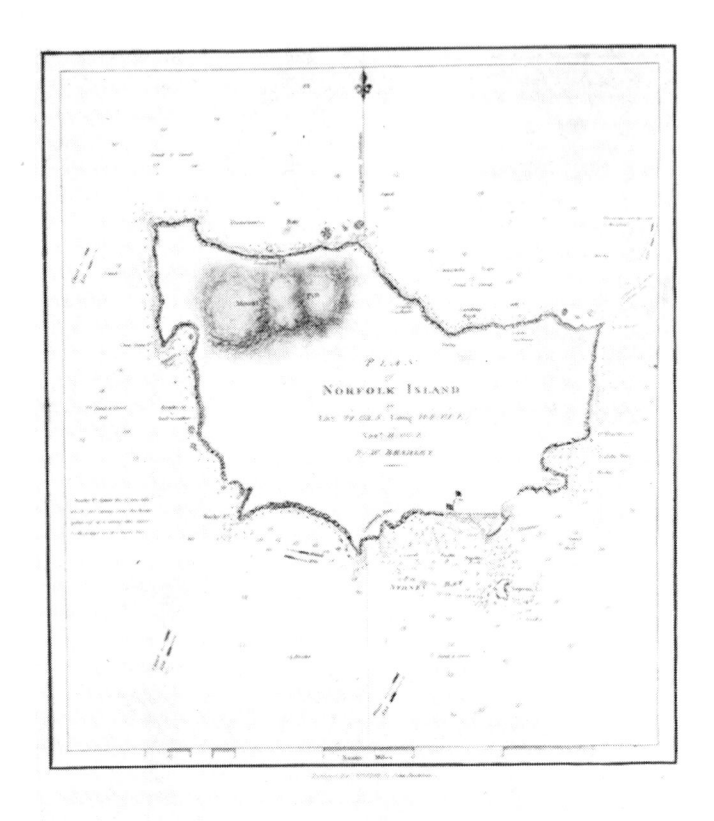

PLAN OF NORFOLK ISLAND
by W. Bradley
From Hunter's Voyage to Botany Bay, *published 1793*

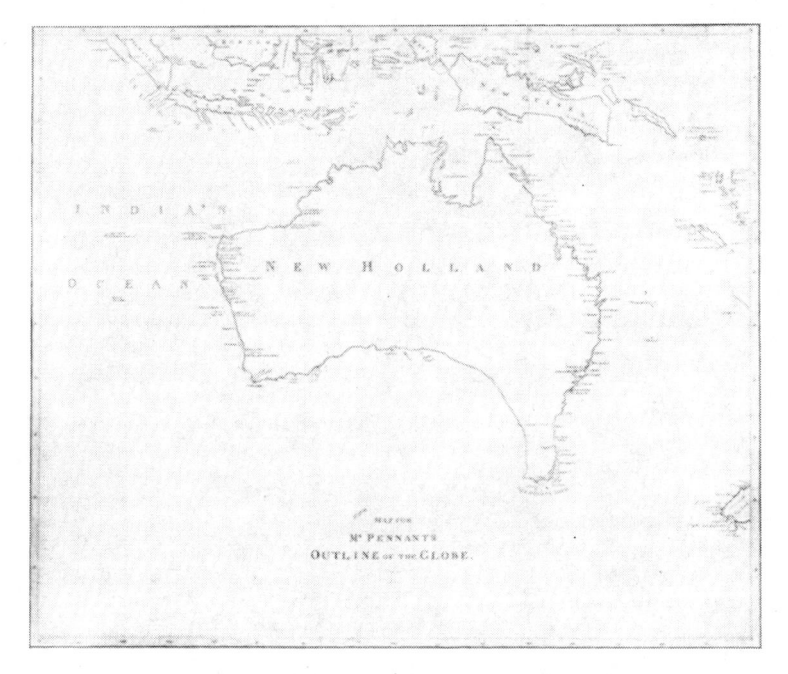

MAP FOR MR. PENNANT'S *OUTLINE OF THE GLOBE*, Vol. IV,
1800

Melbourne Public Library

(Norfolk Island can be seen on the right-hand edge, half-way down)

THE KING FAMILY IN 1799

Governor and Mrs. King with Phillip, Maria, and Elizabeth

Painting by Robert Dighton, English portrait-painter and caricaturist (1752–1814)

In the possession of Sir Philip Goldfinch, Sydney

PAGE ONE OF MRS. KING'S *SPEEDY* DIARY

By permission of the Trustees of the Mitchell Library, Sydney

CAPTAIN PHILLIP PARKER KING

From Fr. Christmann's Australien, *1870*

MRS. HANNIBAL MACARTHUR
(MARIA KING)

Portrait in the possession of Dr. Keith Brown, Parramatta, N.S.W.

THE VINEYARD, PARRAMATTA

After a lithograph by F. C. Terry

By permission of the Trustees of the Mitchell Library, Sydney

CHAPTER V

Life in the Colony
1800–1807

SYDNEY had changed a good deal since Mrs. King had first arrived in the *Gorgon* eight years before. It still had the dimensions of a village (a village, sad to say, nearly denuded of trees), but the rows of small houses, each with its paling fence and little garden, stretched farther up the slopes away from the water's edge. There was still no church steeple, but there was a clock-tower a hundred and fifty feet high, a new stone windmill almost finished to replace the old, 'a handsome and commodious' stone jail, and some new hospital buildings. Government House was no longer the only two-story building—there were two or three others, and a brick granary store of three floors. A bridge crossed the Tank Stream just near the house set apart for Colonel Paterson of the New South Wales Corps, lately returned from England; a few horses and carts were to be seen, and there was more activity in the harbour with locally built schooners plying up the river to Parramatta, coming and going to the Hawkesbury settlement and to Norfolk Island, or bringing coals from Coal River, with an occasional whaler loaded with some hundreds of gallons of whale or sea-elephant oil. There were still the natives coming about, and there were still the convicts employed in gangs or working as assigned servants, as well as those who had completed their sentences and were going freely about their business. Government House itself had been enlarged and now had a veranda overlooking the garden that ran down nearly to the water's edge. In the moments

55

of acutest discomfort on board the *Speedy*, Mrs. King must have thought with longing of the day when she and her husband and Elizabeth could spread their belongings in dry security under that roof. They had arrived, but that day had not yet come.

Their life in the Colony had, in fact, a most uncomfortable beginning. King himself had the ungracious task of delivering to Governor Hunter the dispatches bringing the first news that his reign was over. Hunter, declining an inconveniently early chance of removing himself, preferred to take the colonial ship *Buffalo* to England after refitting her for the voyage. Typically, the refitting took five months and during that time Hunter retained the command, and the occupancy of Government House. King was without power, and his wife without a home. When they first landed, they had to accept an invitation to stay with their old friends the Patersons—very pleasant for the exchanging of reminiscences about the early days shared on Norfolk Island, but where there was no room 'to unpack a box in'. Where they spent the rest of the interval does not appear, but not long after they landed King was hoping 'to get under some shelter in a day or two', and presumably a shelter of sorts was found.

It was a very awkward situation for everybody, not made less so by the inclination of Hunter's enemies amongst the civil and military officers to express their pleasure at the arrival of King: in fact, they preferred the devil they did not know to the devil they did. King, however, was under no delusions; he realized that he would be unpopular as soon as he was in a position to govern the colony as he knew he must. 'I have to root up long-established iniquities,' he wrote. 'I believe this transient satisfaction will soon end with many.' The worst of those iniquities were the unscrupulous trade monopoly exercised by the military, and the all-pervading love of spirits.

King's relations with Hunter grew more strained as the weeks passed, and by June he was writing to London 'I am here enduring the cold indifference of one, and the approaching hatred of all'. The social condition of Sydney perturbed him very much. 'Vice, dissipation, and a strange relaxation seems to pervade every class and order of people.' As to spirits, the 'cellars from the better sort of people in the Colony to the blackest characters amongst the convicts, are full of that fiery poison. The children are abandoned to misery, prostitution, and every vice of their parents, and in short, nothing less than a total change in the system of administration must take place immediately I am left to myself.'

But before he was left to himself many more embarrassing weeks were to pass. Hunter was sore at the manner of his recall; his 'cold indifference' towards his successor soon changed to a jealous hostility and the position, as King said, became painful in the extreme. King, appalled at much that he saw and learnt, and with no jurisdiction except by Hunter's leave, urged him to take certain steps. The suggestions, made though they were with deference, were taken as personal affronts and the offended Governor accused King of acting as a public censor. 'You have not', he told King loftily, 'been long enough in the colony to know what a little more time will give you a more perfect acquaintance with'; to which King, stung at being thus called a new broom, replied that he had had 'a nine year apprenticeship in these colonies'. Finally, Hunter accused King of an indelicate impatience to possess office: King must have longed to reply that Hunter was an unconscionable time dying, but he refrained. Thereafter they were not on speaking terms.

LIFE IN THE COLONY

How unedifying a spectacle for Sydney! And how the settlement's tongues, polite or ribald, must have wagged! Mrs. King, doubtless the uncomfortable recipient of indiscreet or curious comment by the officers' wives, must have longed all the more for walls of her own to shield them both from gossip; longed increasingly for the departure of the *Buffalo* and their own occupation of Government House.

By the end of September Hunter at last went on board. The records do not mention the day or its doings; but private feelings do not cancel official punctilio, and by King's order there will have been a proper showing of scarlet and white on parade, the sounds of fife and drum, of muskets rattling to the salute; a last huzzah for the departing Governor, echoing across the waters of the Cove where the two men, now rivals, had landed on the first day of the settlement as shipmates and friends.

In those early years of Sydney there had been no Governor's wife, for Phillip had left his wife in England and his successor, Hunter, was unmarried; Mrs. King was therefore the first Governor's lady to reign in New South Wales. When at last she saw Hunter embark in the *Buffalo* she must have drawn a long breath of thankfulness: Government House was now hers to command. It was a simple whitewashed house standing on the east side of the Cove and overlooking the harbour. The Kings found it in a sad state of disrepair, needing a new shingle roof and new frames to all the windows and doors; but it was spacious, with a drawing-room nearly as big as the whole of their house on Norfolk Island, a large dining-room leading out of it, and a smaller parlour beyond. Nine windows looked from these rooms across the Cove to the windmills and tower silhouetted against the western sky and to the lovely blue reaches and wooded headlands on the other side of the harbour. A door opened from the dining-room on to the veranda, a stairway led to bedrooms and an attic above.[1] The salt water lapped the rocks below the garden, and the Tank Stream, with its wooden bridge, was only a few hundred yards from their door. Across the bridge, on the parade ground, was the house of their recent hosts, the Patersons; and near it the larger one belonging to Hunter's nephew, Captain Kent; the unpretentious little houses of other officers, the prison buildings, the store, and the cottages of humbler folk, were dotted in rows on either side of the stream; the hospital and surgeons' houses were strung along the western arm of the Cove towards the Observatory on the jutting point. It was a cheerful house for Mrs. King to live in, for nothing was far from her gates and everything could be seen from her veranda—everything except the gallows, which were a short walk from the bridge and mercifully out of sight.

Mrs. King unpacked her boxes and began to keep house. She must have found it difficult to be imaginative in her catering. Salt pork, wheat, and sugar drawn from the public stores, were still the order of the day; there was still anxiety about crops, and the Colony was still a long way from producing stock enough to provide fresh meat. Each shipload of convicts brought nine months' salt meat for those convicts, but when the nine months were over there were just so many more hungry mouths to fill. The cost of all commodities was high, sugar two and six a pound, butter four shillings, soap six, and tobacco ten, and tea £4. 'The common necessaries of life are far, very far, beyond my reach,' wrote King, 'mutton 2s. 6d. a lb. and everything

[1] Ground-floor plan of Government House, *Historical Records, N.S.W.* vi. 764.

else in proportion.' Fish supplies remained uncertain and game in the neighbourhood must have been decreasing. There were more vegetables than before, as there were more free settlers and more land under cultivation, and Government House, with its gardener and two labourers, must have produced at least enough for the household's needs. There was even the occasional luxury of fruit, peaches in particular growing easily. The vines planted after the First Fleet's arrival had promised well and then failed for want of skilled treatment; two French experts had been sent out but the plants they were growing from cuttings would not bear for some years.

When King had been in command a few months and meat rations were getting alarmingly low, with no definite prospect of more arriving from England, he decided to obtain a supply of hogs from the Society Islands. Otaheite's plenteous food was proverbial, from the journals of Captain Cook and the tales of Bligh of the *Bounty* and his mutineers, as well as from the reports of the missionaries who had fled from the island to Sydney a year or two before. A cargo of salt from the Cape having dropped like manna into Port Jackson, brine and casks and gifts to the chief, Pomarré, were dispatched in the *Porpoise* to Otaheite, with Captain Cook's recipe for salting pork. Among the gifts was 'a very elegant scarlet cloth dress made by Mrs. King with her own hands and ornamented in the best manner.'[1] After a few successful 'pork voyages', one of them the last completed enterprise of the famous navigator George Bass,[2] King realized that the island hogs must soon come to an

[1] Missionary Papers, Bonwick Transcripts, Mitchell Library.
[2] Bass sailed again for the South Seas in 1803, planning afterwards a commercial venture on the Spanish South American coasts and a return to Sydney with Chilean cattle. Nothing is definitely known of his end, and in *George Bass* K. McC. Bowden discounts as fable his reputed death in Lima.

LIFE IN THE COLONY

end and his hope of an independent supply of salt meat faded.

Under Hunter, private trading at exorbitant rates had been carried on by the officers of the New South Wales Corps, who imported tea at from 10*s*. to 19*s*. a pound and spirits at 10*s*. a gallon, and sold them at 400 or 500 per cent. advance, as much as £8 a gallon being paid (or owed) for spirits by ex-convict settlers with a rage for drink. As to clothing, weaving was still in its infancy, and its development was still further delayed by the loss of the masterweaver whose drowning was described in her diary by Mrs. King. The officer-farming class, particularly the famous Lieut. John Macarthur, and also the expert farmerchaplain, Marsden, were doing great service by experimenting with the breeding of sheep, crossing the long-haired ewes brought from the Cape with Spanish merino rams. Owners received one out of every four yards of the coarse blanketing that was made from their wool. Less than 700 yards were made in 1801, at a cost of 10*s*. a yard; the industry was indeed in its infancy. Linen-making was on the same scale, and 'of bedding', says King, 'it is much to be regretted that few or none of the labouring people are possessed of the least article', nor was there any bedding to be bought. Clothing, therefore, had all to be imported for the people maintained by the Crown, and for purposes of exchange for the settlers' grain. Shipments were, however, so irregular that a few months before the Kings' arrival Hunter wrote to the Duke of Portland that the colony was in perfect health but 'intirely naked for want of a supply of slop-cloathing and bedding'. On the way out from England Mrs. King had found the contents of her boxes 'in a dismal condition', most of her little things spoilt from lying so long wet in the baggage room of the old *Porpoise*. Ten pounds of calico muslin were lost, and she was thereby 'a few Gowns out of pocket'.[1] Such losses took at best a year to replace, unless by chance the goods could be bought, usually at great cost, at the auction sales of private traders. Articles advertised for sale in this way included such varied items as Gentlemen's Silver Shoebuckles, Norwich Shawls, and Musical instruments; Black, green and white Persians and Lute strings, Ladies' Spanish leather and Morocco shoes; Snuff boxes in ivory and amber; Gentlemen's superfine beaver hats of the latest description; black and green tea; Fowling pieces and jaconet muslins; Ink powder and wafers and ready made pens:[2]—small comfort, all this, to people in want of regular supplies of plain things in daily use. King had left with his agent a list of a few miscellaneous articles to be sent out to him each year, including Souchong tea, sugar, thirty-six dozen of port wine, the *European Magazine* and a guinea's worth of pins:[3] these cannot have gone far towards solving the house-keeping problem. Occasional friends going overseas were helpful. There is a letter from Mrs. King to Mr. D'Arcy Wentworth, thanking him with many italics for the very *pretty bonnet* he had procured for her, so *exactly* to her *choice*, and also for the gift of a neat little bonnet for the seven-year-old Elizabeth.[4]

Assigned servants from the well-behaved convicts were obtainable at £10 a year, and rationed from the stores, but the number of these was limited. Most of the women convicts, King said, were 'of the worst description and totally irreclaimable being generally the refuse of London', and the decent country ones were employed spinning. Mrs. King brought one servant from England, the Jane Dundas who injured herself on the voyage, and seems to have had

[1] Mrs. King's *Speedy* Diary.
[2] *Sydney Gazette.*
[3] *King Papers.*
[4] *Wentworth Papers.*

LIFE IN THE COLONY

at least two others at Government House, whether free women imported as servants, or assigned or emancipated convicts, does not appear. King had a coxswain and eight men for his boat, a bodyguard of six privates and a non-commissioned officer selected from the New South Wales Corps, and another of five provisionally emancipated convicts of good character who were mounted and used to trot behind the Governor's coach[1] as it swung behind four horses along the roads between Sydney and the outlying settlements that grew in number under King.

Of his many problems, the neglected children seemed to the new Governor the most urgent. In Norfolk Island King had seen to it that the children had all the care and teaching that he could provide.[2] In Sydney nothing whatever had been done; now Governor and Mrs. King set to work together to help the waifs who, they felt, were the future hope of the Colony. There were nine hundred and fifty-eight of them, a large proportion of whom were illegitimate.[3] King said roundly that 'finer or more neglected children were not to be met with in any part of the world. A roomy brick house near the Bridge had lately been built for Captain Kent, who was returning to England; this house King bought, and the owner made a gift of the garden planted with fruit trees valued by himself at about £300. The property was to be an orphanage for the entire seclusion of a hundred little girls, who were either real orphans or the children of undesirable parents. King invited six people to act as a committee of management—probably the first committee

---

[1] The coach and emancipist bodyguard can be seen in a picture entitled 'View of Sydney Cove, New South Wales,' published in London, April 1804, from a picture painted in the colony.

[2] King's *Journal*.

[3] Six years later, when the number was 1808, half were illegitimate. *Historical Records, N.S.W.* vi. 151 and 152.

63

in Australian history—and two of the members were Mrs. King and Mrs. Paterson. The others were the two clergymen, Johnson and Marsden, and two surgeons, Harris and Balmain, all four of whom were magistrates. Another orphanage was to be built in Parramatta, and after these institutions for girls were in working order something was to be done for the boys.

This activity, which was of real importance in the social development of the settlement, became known as 'Mrs. King's Orphanage', for it was one of her greatest interests and absorbed much of her time. At the first meeting the Committee found themselves with certain assets in cash and kind (the kind including two leggers of brandy, 304 gallons in the public store), opened a subscription list, and ordered an estimate to be got for the quantity of planks and scantling necessary for fifty bed cradles 5 ft. by 3 ft. to hold two children each. The artificers were to be paid in salt meat, tobacco, and rum.

The opening ceremony a year later began with a sermon preached by the vigorous Mr. Marsden, who gave a true description of the parents of the children, with the children sitting in the congregation before him. Later, says an admiring missionary recently arrived from Otaheite,

'The Rev. Mr. Marsden conducted us to the Orphan House (which is the best house in all Sydney, none excepted) where we was highly delighted with seeing the girls in the greatest order feasting on excellent salt pork and plum pudding, and seemed very happy in their new situation. The daily visitors are Mrs. King and Mrs. Paterson, the two first ladies in rank in the Colony.'

The children were taught needlework, spinning, and reading, and some of them writing also. They were victualled by the Crown, but all other expenses were met from

LIFE IN THE COLONY

the proceeds from fines and forfeits, from shipping dues ear-marked for the purpose, and a 5 per cent. duty on foreign goods. Mrs. King and Mrs. Paterson both devoted themselves to the supervision of the orphanage, which according to a contemporary account acted as a training-ground for virtuous wifehood, with Mrs. King in the capacity of a matrimonial agent armed with the powers of refusal and consent.[1]

This work was of greater importance than, from the small number of the inmates, one might suppose. The convict women of Sydney, said King, were most of them beyond reclamation by kindness or punishment, apart from the few who came from the English counties; but excepting the most abandoned, he did not believe in shutting them up—it was more practical to shut up the rising generation. Among the convict women matrimony was not usual. When King had been in command for some years, while there were nine thousand souls in the whole colony there were only three hundred and sixty married couples.[2]

---

[1] François Péron, naturalist of the Baudin Expedition, in his report to Decaen on the Settlement at Port Jackson. Speaking of the labours of Mrs. King and Mrs: Paterson, he says: 'Chacune d'elles ou toutes les deux ensemble vont exactement visiter tous les jours leur jeune famille, comme elles disent elles-même. Elles ne négligent rien pour assurer la propreté, l'instruction et la bonne qualité des alimens. J'ai plusieurs fois accompagné les deux respectables dames, dans cet Établissement, et j'ai chaque fois été vivement ému de leur solicitude quiète et de leur soins touchants.'

Péron ill repaid the hospitality of the Kings, the Patersons, and the other leading people of the Colony. The expedition, protected by a British passport, was undoubtedly purely a scientific one, and Péron was a very fine scientist; nevertheless in his report to Decaen he states that he used the chances given him by his unsuspecting hosts to find out all he could that might be useful from a political or would-be conqueror's point of view. His report, checked against other contemporary accounts, gives a much too glowing picture of the state of the settlement at the time—it was seen with the eyes of envy, looking through rose-coloured spectacles.

[2] *Historical Records, N.S.W.* vi. 151, 290.

'It certainly would be desirable', King wrote, 'if marriage were more prevalent, as every encouragement is given for their entering into that state; but as the will of individuals ought, in this instance, to be free, I cannot say that I ever approved of a proposed plan to lock all the females up who are not married until they are so fortunate as to obtain husbands. Every proper precaution is taken by putting the females on their arrival into the manufactory ... from whence the well-behaved are selected and applied for by settlers and others to become their housekeepers or servants; and the incorrigible are kept confined to the manufactory, where they have no communication with the men, or sent to the coal works at Newcastle.'

To attempt their segregation would, he averred, have the same results as persecution for religious opinion—it would merely increase the evil. But where the children and young girls were concerned, segregation was what he did attempt and in this work Mrs. King was his chief assistant.

Sydney had its echo of the Jacobin movement in the Old Country, its group of respectable English and Scottish political prisoners, 'Friends of the People', who had been transported for no more than wanting a vote and organizing peaceably to get it. Soon after the Irish Rebellion of 1798, however, a new element appeared among those sent out for sedition—a more difficult element, the United Irish. Some of them were educated, or at least intelligent, among their number their late leader, the flamboyant 'General' Joseph Holt; more of them were ignorant and bitterly resentful of the horrors of the '98 and desperate enough to risk a blow for freedom at any time. The best of them were unamenable, the worst an alarming addition to a colony already composed chiefly of people who were unsatisfactory from one point of view or another. In any case a British Protestant community was at that time more than ready to take fright at anything a Catholic might do; so that there was enough of both fact and fancy to explain the mood of a letter that Mrs. Paterson had written to England just before the Kings arrived. 'The first cargo of rebels are arrived in the *Minerva*, they are already begun to concert schemes.' ' We certainly are at present nearly as uncomfortable and harassed as the people in Ireland were at the time of the Rebellion.... For the last six months we have been under some apprehensions.' Governor Hunter, she says, had not believed that trouble was brewing and had taken no steps for the protection of the people. But on the previous Sunday a plan had been discovered for 'the destruction of the military and the principal families in Parramatta, and thirty of the most desperate were taken up and confessed the whole plot'.

Soon after King's arrival there was rumour of an intention to kill him and confine Hunter. With fearful quill Mrs. Paterson now writes: 'I have no idea myself that they will ever appear in numbers or in noonday—my terror is private assassination, breaking into our houses in the dead of night.'[1]

Mrs. Paterson was not the only one to suffer from apprehension; the whole of Sydney lived in a constant state of suspicion of the 'violent Republicans' and prepared to defend themselves by enrolling as volunteers in the specially formed Loyal Associations, drilled by sergeants of the New South Wales Corps. Not to be nervous in these circumstances was more than could be expected of feminine flesh and blood, and Mrs. King, no less than Mrs. Paterson, must have shaken in her shoes. But after a while the public fear of the Irish simmered down; King, ever fair-minded, conditionally emancipated one of their number to allow of his exercising his duties as a priest, mass being conducted for the first time in the history of the Colony. Trouble of a sort continued amongst them, but King, not expecting their

[1] Mitchell Library MSS.

'ridiculous plans' for seizing the settlement to 'go beyond conversation', and anxious to get on with harvesting and other useful activities, disbanded the Loyal Associations of Volunteers.

And then—a whisper of trouble, a warning disregarded as a case of 'wolf', and at last the reality, the night alarm that was Mrs. Paterson's dread. Late one Sunday Governor King got word of an uprising at Castle Hill, near Parramatta. The alarm was given and ten minutes later the soldiers and inhabitants were under arms. King put Paterson in charge of Sydney and leaping on his horse rode off for Parramatta unattended through the dark. For nearly a week Mrs. King had to endure her wifely fears, with news filtering back into Sydney of armed mobs clashing with the red coats, of shouts of Death or Liberty! of summary executions, floggings, and chains.[1] King, obliged to hang many during that ugly week, forgave where he could—indeed, according to Sir Joseph Banks, his only fault as a Governor was a tendency to forgive far too often.[2] A different type of man, tortured with gout as King was, might have fed the gallows, but despite his bad health King kept his merciful nature and, Sir Joseph or no Sir Joseph, one feels that his wife preferred it so.

Some months after their arrival the Kings had a delightful surprise. A vessel had come in from Norfolk Island; and suddenly in walked William Chapman, come to see how they were getting on. They pelted him with questions about the Island, and King at once appointed him to a post at the Stores that would allow him a certain amount of time to act as his private secretary.[3] Since King's promulga-

---
[1] *Sydney Gazette*, vol. ii, no. 54.
[2] *Banks Papers*, Brabourne Collection, iv. 168–71.
[3] *Chapman Papers*.

tion of an order from the Duke of York, the Army's Commander-in-Chief, that 'all manner of traffic in spirituous liquors particularly is forbidden to any person bearing H.M.'s Commission in the Colony', King's public life had, as he expected, become very difficult and his private life often very unpleasant—a condition that also affected the female friendships of Mrs. King. Except his aide-de-camp Lieut. McKellar, there was nobody, Chapman told his family, whom the Governor could trust to help him deal with the multiplicity of requests, complaints, and appeals that together with his responsibility for the civil, judicial, and military administration of a growing territory, and the crises that happened from time to time, gave King, as he said himself, full employment for the whole of his time, and every exertion of his body and mind. The renewal of Chapman's secretarial services was providential, and his loyal friendship a solace for the criticism and even calumny that grew more and more rife. He was allotted a little whitewashed cottage close to Government House, but, as in Norfolk Island, he was one of King's family circle and spent much of his time under their roof.

All the more disturbing, then, to both the Governor and his wife must have been an episode two or three years later, typical of Sydney's many storms in tea-cups, that caused King to suspend his young friend and secretary until it was settled whether Chapman or the naval captain of a visiting ship was the liar in the case. Captain Colnett of H.M.S. *Glatton* was of higher naval rank than the Governor of the Colony and considered that in Port Jackson he was treated as 'a master to a petty coaster'; he felt, too, that his ship had been meanly treated in the matter of fresh beef, whereas King thought that 775 lb. in eight weeks was 'a cheerful but costly supply in so young a colony'. There were other matters of dispute; but what undoubtedly enraged Colnett more than questions of rank or rations was King's refusal to risk his own ruin by misusing his official powers in favour of a convict girl who had lived with Colnett on the voyage. Colnett wanted a free pardon for her so that she could return with him in the *Glatton*; King pointed out that the official recommendation for the Governor's free pardon that Colnett had been influential enough to obtain even before leaving England, was conditional on the girl's behaving well for twelve months after landing in Sydney, and Colnett had not yet landed her from his ship: King was, in fact, unable to pardon a convict not yet delivered to him, nor had he power to do so until after she had been in the settlement for a year.[1]

Finally, there was a question of the ship's papers being in order before the *Glatton* was allowed to sail: it was in this matter that Chapman became embroiled. If Colnett was irascible, Chapman was rash. Denying an accusation against him by Colnett, he declared publicly in a written statement 'that Captain Colnett, or any other person who dares to say that ever I gave it out publicly and officially as secretary to His Excellency Governor King, that the *Glatton* was to sail at any particular time, is a liar, a scoundrell, and a vagabond; and that whoever he is, if he has the spirit to come forward, that I will wring his nose and spit in his face'.

Glorious!

King told Colnett that Chapman was 'a person whom I have ever been proud to call my confidential secretary and friend'; nevertheless, in view of Colnett's standing (and

---

[1] The girl in question was granted a conditional emancipation in 1804 by King, and in 1810 Macquarie emancipated her absolutely. *Historical Records, N.S.W.* v. 97 note.

LIFE IN THE COLONY

possibly in part as a rebuke to Chapman for the gusto of his denial) the Governor suspended him until it could be settled which of the two gentlemen was the 'scoundrell'. Next day, Chapman, 'deprived of his bread' by Colnett's aspersion, requested the constitution of a Civil Court to consider his appeal for redress, and assessed the damages at £10,000. On the same day, Colnett, not so conversant as Chapman with legal procedure, demanded that the young man be brought before a Criminal Court. King sent the Judge-Advocate on board the *Glatton* to explain that Chapman was not indictable criminally but that an action would lie in the Civil Court. Colnett, still blustering, demanded that Chapman be either sent Home or held in disgrace until a decision could be made in England. King would have none of this: a Civil Court, he told Colnett, would be instituted at nine o'clock the following morning; if Colnett took no action, the omission would be enough cause for Chapman's reinstatement in office. The Captain hedged: protesting that his cause was of too serious a nature to come before a Civil Court, he vowed that nothing but wind and weather would delay his departure beyond the next morning. H.M.S. *Glatton* swept out of the harbour next day, and if there had been a door at the Heads one feels that her commander would have banged it. A few months later he was in London pouring poison into official ears.

It is allowable to assume Chapman's immediate reinstatement, but the Kings were not to have his friendly company for long. In 1804 he went to England on leave, writing thence affectionately to Mrs. King to describe Maria, now 'a nice sprightly girl' a good deal like her mother, and Phillip, who had grown into 'such a lovely boy'. William wished to be remembered to the faithful Dundas, now the Kings' housekeeper, and sent instructions to 'the darling little Elizabeth' that she must be able to read and write perfectly by July or August next, when he expected to be back in Sydney once more.

Sad to say, the Kings never saw Chapman again. Changing his plans, from England he went to seek his fortune in the East as a trader between Madras and Port Jackson. Fortune eluded him. After six years in Madras, without the hoped-for trip to Port Jackson, he lost his money through dishonest associates in a trading concern. He then settled in Java, where he grew coffee, pineapples and sugar, and made rum; he also had interests in Batavia. He was about sixty-four years old when he died, shattered in health and apparently no better off than when as a lad he had worked for King for an annual salary of £50.[1] Poor warm-hearted William! Did he sometimes think of those almost idyllic days on Norfolk Island, more than forty years before?

Colnett's bitter tales of the Governor were not the only ones that were told, for it was not to be expected that in that community and in that age people in the position of the Kings could escape from attack by scurrilous tongues. There is in the Records a long letter from an Irish convict to Lord Castlereagh giving details of alleged corrupt practices by both the Governor and his wife, who are supposed to have bartered free pardons in exchange for jewellery and fine lace. There was a Frenchman known in Sydney as Meurant who had been transported for attempting to defraud the Bank of Dublin in 1798 and who received a free pardon in June 1803. Castlereagh's informer claimed that Meurant had never done any work of public utility but had been employed all his time in making jewellery and trinkets for Mrs. King; that another notorious resident, a receiver of stolen goods, had made a gift to her of 'some

[1] *Chapman Papers.*

superlatively fine lace' formerly the property of the Marchioness of Salisbury and presented the Governor himself with 'a very curious watch of immense value' stolen from the Count d'Artois. He asserted that the Governor, from belated panic, had withheld from the 'fence' the pardon that was to have been the reward of his bribes and banished the writer of the letter to Norfolk Island for knowing—and talking—too much.

More credible tales than this one were probably ignored by the Home Department when their authors were convicts; this libellous letter, composed with such care by the Irish exile, will have done no more than brighten the dull morning of some Whitehall clerk. Its only value is that it gives a glimpse of the sort of thing that the Governor of a penal colony had to put up with, and shows that his wife cannot without danger to her reputation even indulge an innocent feminine love of lace and precious stones.

King was an honest believer in the value of religious observances, therefore we can be quite sure that on Sundays he and his family attended church regularly, although during their régime there was, strictly speaking, no church to attend. In Governor Phillip's time, the Rev. Richard Johnson, after more than five years of preaching under trees or in odd corners, disgusted at official apathy, built a small wooden structure at his own expense. The cost was £67. 13s. 2½d. and was not refunded without argument and many years' delay. This wattle and plaster shelter served for another five years and was large enough to house the small congregation on Sundays and serve as a school house for about two hundred children during the week. But the officers were lax church-goers, and among the humbler inhabitants there was a distressing, but surely not surprising, indifference to the Sabbath Day. Finally Governor Hunter appealed to the officers, civil and military, and commanded the convicts, to appear every Sunday at divine service. The command had quick results: within a few weeks 'some wicked and disaffected person or persons . . . took an opportunity of a windy and dark evening and set fire to the church'. Hunter counter-moved by fitting up a newly finished weather-board store-house as a temporary place for public worship and laying the foundations of large stone churches at Sydney and Parramatta. But founding is one thing and finishing another; there were few skilled artificers and many utilitarian works to be done: the store remained Sydney's only church until St. Philip's was completed in 1809. It was to this store that the Kings repaired on Sundays, to listen to their old acquaintance the evangelical Mr. Johnson until he left the colony with Governor Hunter in 1800; and presumably it was this building that first housed the silver communion service sent in 1803 by George III 'for the use of the Chapel at His Majesty's Settlement at Sydney, New South Wales'. This and the prayer book and Bible used at the first service, February 3rd, 1788, are now in St. Philip's, Wynyard Square, Sydney.

After Johnson's departure, the vigorous Mr. Marsden took the service at Sydney on Sunday mornings and at Parramatta in the afternoons. Like Johnson, he was of an evangelical persuasion, and both were farmers—being obliged, in the state of the Colony 'to plant and sow, or starve'; Johnson grew the first oranges from seed from Rio and Marsden, with Macarthur, the first fine-quality wool. After twelve years of unhappy service, Johnson retired beaten to the obscurity of an English village: Marsden's greater courage kept him a fiery missioner in the new world until his death. King, early in his rule, confirmed Hunter's orders on the observance of the Sabbath and attendance at

LIFE IN THE COLONY

church, and instructed the sentinels and watchmen to confine all people found strolling about Sydney and Parramatta during the hours of divine service.... Yes, indeed, it seems quite certain that Mr. Marsden, surveying from his pulpit on Sunday morning the gathering below him of the willing and the unwilling, rarely missed the upturned faces of Mrs. King and even of the little Elizabeth, sitting dutifully beside the Governor, their domestic retinue respectfully behind.

In 1803 King started Australia's first newspaper, the *Sydney Gazette and New South Wales Advertizer*, a weekly that was designed to benefit the inhabitants by disseminating useful information. 'We open no channel to Political Discussion or Personal Animadversion', announced its editor, an 'ingenious' convict and later the Government printer, George Howe; indeed, in a place where ink was so frequently mixed with vitriol, the veto was essential, and in Sydney at that time the plain facts were often sensational enough. Howe collected the material; the Governor's secretary inspected it each week,[1] and the settlement was enlivened with the result every Sunday. In London there was a demand for them, as Chapman found when he went there on leave. Copies of the *Gazette*, he wrote to Mrs. King, were 'in very great repute, and looked upon as great curiosities'. He asked her to tell the Governor that the Under-Secretary wanted all the back numbers and in future twelve complete sets were to be sent to England by every ship. Five reams of printing paper were to be sent out to the printer to enable him to go on with the *Gazette*. Banks, too, wanted them sent regularly, though, true scientist, he regretted the impossibility of an opposition press to put the other side.

Life had its lighter-hearted days, and the *Gazette* its

[1] *Historical Records of Australia*, Series I, iv. 662.

LIFE IN THE COLONY

social gossip as well as its belated news of the war with France, its paragraphs about the progress of the new church, the work on the stone bridge over the Tank Stream, its Lists of Free Pardons and Emancipations, its accounts of shipping, of drought and flood. His Majesty's birthday was always festively honoured; there were vice-regal dinner-parties at three in the afternoon, followed by splendid balls, elegant fêtes, and brilliant fireworks. When troops were about to embark with prisoners for the intended settlement in Van Diemen's Land there was dining and dancing at Government House in honour of the officers and their wives, and on the day that the expedition sailed H.E. the Governor and the Ladies accompanied the ships down the harbour, while bands played and the crowd cheered. There were excursions by land in which Mrs. King and sometimes the Patersons joined the Governor, and one red-letter day a 'Partie', including Mrs. King, managed 'without much fatigue' to penetrate as far as the Nepean River, about twenty-four miles from Parramatta. 'At daylight the morning following His Excellency attended by several Gentlemen, crossed the River, and proceeded towards the place chiefly resorted to by the Wild Cattle. The river was passed and repassed several times in the course of the day by Mrs. King, who, we may confidently affirm, is the first and only Lady that has ever crossed the Nepean'. Mrs. King, then, could ride, and trackless bush and wild bulls did not deter her.

CHAPTER VI

Friends, Feuds, and Foreigners
1800–1807

THE time of King's governorship was an era of expansion. Only a few miles to the west of Sydney the Blue Mountains continued to act as an impenetrable barrier to runaway convicts who believed that China lay just on the other side, and to the herd of ferocious wild cattle that were the descendants of those that had strayed in the days of Governor Phillip.[1] But by sea there was much exploration, and Mrs. King was hostess and friend to men whose names are famous in the history of Australian discovery. One of these who frequented Government House in 1802 and 1803 was Matthew Flinders. When he left he wrote his thanks to both the Governor and 'my dear friend Mrs. King' for kindness too great for words to express, and sent messages to 'my little Elizabeth'. Poor Flinders! He had planned to bring his wife out to Port Jackson in the *Investigator* and to leave her there while he carried out his survey of the coast; there, he says, she also would have become a friend of Mrs. King. Just after their marriage in England, unsuccessfully kept secret, she lived on board with him for several weeks, and was indiscreet enough to be seen by an Admiralty official sitting in the cabin with her bonnet off. Sea-faring wives were anathema to that influential patron of scientific discovery, the great Sir Joseph Banks; Flinders was warned by Banks that if he took his bride to New South Wales he would certainly be superseded and the survey finished by another officer.[2] Flinders wrote the most

[1] Appendix II.   [2] *Flinders Papers.*

77

heart-broken letters to his poor wife, but assured Sir Joseph that if necessary he would 'give up the wife for the voyage of discovery'. Sir Joseph talked of 'the laxity of discipline that always takes place when the Captain's wife is on board'; the Admiralty remained stony-hearted: the wife was given up. From Sydney, Flinders wrote to her:
'Thou wouldst have been situated as comfortably here as I hoped, and told thee. Two better or more agreeable women than Mrs. King and Mrs. Paterson are not easily found; these would have been thy choicest friends, and for visiting acquaintances there are five or six other ladies, very agreeable for short periods and perhaps longer.'[1]

Again he writes to her on the King's birthday:
'This is a great day in all distant British settlements, and we are preparing to celebrate it with due magnificence. The ship is covered with colours, and every man is about to put on his best apparel, and to make himself merry. We go through the form of waiting upon His Excellency the Governor at his *levee*, to pay our compliments to him as representative of Majesty. After which a dinner and ball are given to the Colony at which not less than 52 gentlemen and ladies will be present.'

And he adds how much rather he would have a 'right hand and left' at the house of his loved cousins, the Franklins, than all the formality which they were to go through that evening.

He writes again of the attention that he has received from the Governor and his 'kind friend Mrs. King'. The letter was to the wife of his great friend, Captain Kent, who was then in Sydney.

'It is', he adds, 'a cause of much uneasiness to me that Colonel and Mrs. Paterson should be on terms of disagreement with them' (i.e. the Kings). 'There is now Mrs. King and Mrs. Paterson and Mrs. McArthur for all of whom I have the greatest

[1] *Flinders Papers.*

regard, who can scarcely speak to each other; it is really a miserable thing to split a small society into such small parts; why do you ladies meddle with politics?'[1]

A foolish question to ask! At the time of Flinders's letter, happy relations between the three wives could hardly be expected, for Mrs. Macarthur's husband was in England, sent home under arrest by Mrs. King's husband for having dangerously wounded Mrs. Paterson's husband in a duel. Moreover, although the duel had originated in a purely regimental squabble, the names of all three ladies had been mentioned by the disputants; Macarthur had been accused of improperly handing about a letter from Mrs. Paterson to his wife, and there had been hints that Mrs. Paterson might use her friendship with Mrs. King to influence the Governor against Macarthur. No, the ladies were kept apart, not by politics, but by personalities. As often as their husbands could mend their quarrels, eat their violent words, call off their duels, just so often could the wives once more meet amicably under each other's roofs or while going the rounds of the Orphanage.

Storms brewed naturally in the neighbourhood of the tempestuous John Macarthur. Spiked words came more easily than smooth ones to that impulsive tongue. If he thought a man a liar he said so, in writing, and was quite likely to add that he was a black traitor, a miscreant, and a poltroon. It was not in him to compromise, to be anybody's obedient servant, and peaceable relations between himself and his fellow officers, or with the Governor—any Governor—were hard to maintain. When later Bligh took over the Colony from King, an explosion with Macarthur was inevitable: King was an easier man than Bligh, but, even with King, Macarthur was constantly at war. Macarthur,

[1] *Matthew Flinders, Private Letters,* Mitchell Library MSS.

however, was not just a firebrand and an egoist, noted for his quarrels and his resistance to authority: he was one of the country's most valuable settlers, because he was intelligent enough to see that Australia must find an export if she was not to be a burden on England for ever, and imaginative enough to realize that the obvious export commodity was wool. Not wool as it then generally was in the colony, but wool as he and Samuel Marsden had proved that it could become. He spent his compulsory visit to England in interesting the Government and manufacturers in his project, and returned with Lord Camden's promise of a large grant of land in an area chosen by Macarthur himself, in return for undertaking to change the colonial flocks of hair-bearing sheep into producers of fine wool equal to the best fleeces of Spain. King, rebuked for his action in sending Macarthur to England, shook hands with 'the hero of the fleece' and sent an amusing account of the reconciliation to one of Macarthur's many enemies and the opponent of his wool schemes, Sir Joseph Banks.[1]

King and Macarthur were to disagree again, but there were recurring interludes of friendship and later a union of the two families through marriage. In the meantime, Mrs. King must surely have regretted a breach as often as it occurred, for Mrs. Macarthur was as distinctive a character as her husband and worth having as a friend. Just before the two women had first met as young wives in 1791, Mrs. Macarthur had been lamenting that she had not employment for her idle hours. 'Anxious to learn some easy science to fill up the vacuum' of her days, she was dabbling in astronomy and botany with Lieut. Dawes and learning from Mr. Worgan, surgeon of the *Sirius*, how to play Foot's Minuet and 'God Save the King' upon the piano that he had brought with

[1] *The Macarthurs of Camden*, p. 110.

him across the world.[1] Those days were over. There was more than enough scope for her energy and intelligence in sharing the management of Elizabeth Farm, Parramatta, where the Macarthurs had been living for some years, and where, for the first time in the history of the country, a plough was used. Later, after the rebellion against Bligh in which Macarthur played a leading part that resulted in his leaving the Colony, and before her sons were old enough to help her, Mrs. Macarthur carried alone and successfully the burdens of their estate and affairs while her husband chafed in England for more than eight years awaiting the permission of the Home Government to return. Those burdens were such that, as the grateful Macarthur himself wrote to her, 'not one women in a thousand ... would have resolution and perseverance to contend with them at all, much more to surmount them in the manner you have so happily done'. Their absence from each other was a cruel break in their lives. Many years afterwards, Mrs. Macarthur owned to a sympathetic interest in the Pitcairn Islanders, descendants of the Bounty Mutineers, who, she felt, were victims, like her husband, of the 'tyranny' of Bligh.

A breach with the Macarthurs was a vexation to Governor and Mrs. King but estrangement from the Patersons must have really hurt. Macarthur, through the force of his own character, counted for more in the community than Paterson, but even in his cordial moments was never an intimate friend of King's. Paterson, in his dual capacity of Lieutenant Governor and Commanding Officer of the New South Wales Corps, was a colleague who came into contact with King every day; moreover they had been colleagues before, on Norfolk Island, where for fifteen months Paterson had been King's right-hand man, and his wife Mrs. King's only

[1] *The Macarthurs of Camden*, pp. 498, 499.

available woman friend. Also, King and Paterson shared an interest in scientific pursuits, for the Governor was full of the untrained curiosity of the period and place, and Paterson, who owed his commission in the Corps to Sir Joseph Banks,[1] had done some notable exploration in Africa and was, in fact, more of a naturalist than a soldier. Now, King criticized Paterson for being too easily influenced by the intrigues of his subordinate officers—meaning Macarthur in particular—and Paterson took offence from the 'too hasty and unguarded expressions' used by his Chief; relations between the two men became more and more strained and in the end their wives, as Flinders lamented, could scarcely speak to each other.

Feuds did not come easily to Mrs. King; loyal wife as she always was, she must have had a pang for the friendship of that first strange year on Norfolk Island, when everything was new, including her baby, and much of it was alarming; when Mrs. Paterson was there to share walks and gossip by day, and at night was linked to her by the patrol between their two gardens pacing from fence to fence with muskets loaded and orders to fire on intruders 'with an intention not to miss'. Yes, in those early days of difficulty and even danger their husbands had not quarrelled; but then, John Macarthur was not on the Island. There was a great deal in King's view that Paterson was weak and Macarthur his evil genius.

In 1804 King sent Paterson to establish a post on the Van Diemen's Land shore of Bass Straits, in anticipation of settlement by the French. Complying with the counsel, kind but firm, of their mutual patron, Sir Joseph Banks, the two British officers shook hands for the good of a colony menaced, they thought, by Napoleon's designs. After that

[1] *Australian Encyclopedia.*

the letters that they exchanged grew warmer in tone; Paterson sent Mrs. King a gift of Van Diemen's Land birds as 'the only small acknowledgement' he could offer 'for the many marks of her friendship' to his wife and himself; and Mrs. King pleased Paterson with a 'kind present' of corned beef.

Paterson was still at his post when King was succeeded by Bligh; soon after, as Lieutenant-Governor of the Colony, he was involved in the turmoil following Bligh's arrest and, returning to Sydney, was once more dominated by Macarthur and his fellow conspirators against Bligh. The ship that brought Sydney its new governor, Macquarie, took the ineffectual Paterson away, shattered in health, and he died near Cape Horn on the voyage home.

When some months later Mrs. Paterson left the ship in England, after an absence of nineteen years broken only once by a visit home, it was Macarthur who offered her his escort from Portsmouth to London. He had himself arrived a year before to do battle with ex-Governor Bligh, and hearing of the arrival of ships from Sydney had hastened to Portsmouth for the latest news of the Colony. In a letter to his wife, he expressed some complacence in making his gallant offer to Mrs. Paterson, the widow of the man who had challenged him to a duel. Mrs. Paterson, he said, appeared to be 'grateful for this mark of attention', but one may suppose that in accepting his escort she in her turn felt she was heaping coals of fire on Macarthur's head. After all, it was her husband, not Macarthur, who had been seriously wounded in the duel, and Macarthur had provoked the challenge partly by malicious talk about Mrs. Paterson herself. Probably, as homesick colonials, they were more than glad of each other's company and glad to let bygones be bygones.

Macarthur told his wife that Mrs. Paterson was in good health and excellent spirits. Poor Mrs. Paterson—she had for so long watched her husband going physically downhill and, it was widely said, relying more and more upon drink, that his death may have been a relief. Not long after, she married General Francis Grose, once Paterson's senior in the New South Wales Corps and the man who, while acting-Governor, so severely censured King for accompanying the kidnapped Maoris home to New Zealand.

When very soon Mrs. Paterson was widowed again, it was to Mrs. King she turned for comfort, Mrs. King who rescued her from her lonely house and gave her shelter until she was able to face the world once more. When that time came, Mrs. King and the blossoming young Elizabeth spent many weeks at a time with 'dear Mrs. Grose' in *delightful Bath*.[1] There, drinking the waters or watching Elizabeth whirling in the fashionable new Waltz, the two women must have spent many hours talking over old times. And the time that, looked back on, counted for least, was probably that period of estrangement of which Flinders had written in exasperation to his wife.

In one of King's letters to Paterson in Van Diemen's Land, he gave three melancholy items of news. One was the failure of the harvest, one was his own bad health, and the third was the grave illness of the Kings' housekeeper, Jane Dundas. As to the last, 'poor Dundas', replied Paterson, 'I am sure you will never get such another'. How came humble Jane to be a topic of conversation between governors? She had been transported from London in 1788, for some crime unrecorded but undoubtedly small, as the sentence was for the minimum length of seven years. Two years later she became housemaid to Governor Phillip

[1] *Piper Correspondence*, i. 295.

FRIENDS, FEUDS, AND FOREIGNERS

and when he left for England she remained with acting-Governors Grose and Paterson. Still in service, she returned to England, probably in the *Britannia* in 1796 with either the Patersons or the Kings, and with the Kings she came back to Sydney in the *Speedy* in 1800. When she died, the Kings lamented 'the loss of an honest, faithful and affectionate servant', and did her honour in the eyes of Sydney by attending her funeral 'accompanied by several officers and persons of the first respectability'. Botany Bay, so grim a spectre, had proved kind to Dundas. As she had sat in the pleasant comfort of the housekeeper's room, with her own writing-desk and her books and the treasures of her sewing outfit close at hand, did she sometimes contrast it all with the squalor of the crowded transport and remember the bitterness of being one of that crowd? Or had the grateful affection of Governor and Mrs. King, the love of little Elizabeth, wiped from her mind all memory of those unhappy far-off days of the First Fleet?[1]

In Australia's past, international incidents figured little, but in 1802 one occurred that adds grace to the somewhat stark history of those days and exemplifies again the kindliness of both the Kings. Flinders had explored the South Coast, and on his return to Sydney sat down in his cabin in the *Investigator* to write to Sir Joseph Banks. He tells him that after he had finished the most interesting part of the coast he had met the French explorer, Baudin, in the *Géographe,* carrying out a scientific survey for Napoleon; that Baudin said he had found no ports, harbours, or inlets, nor had he seen a certain large island; that after Baudin's account of the coast it had surprised Flinders not a little to find in the mainland opposite this island a very large port; but that Flinders himself was not the discoverer of either

[1] *Sydney Gazette*, December 22nd and 29th, 1805, and March 30th, 1806.

port or island, for on returning to Sydney he found that Lieut. Murray of the *Lady Nelson* had discovered and named both. These were King Island, in Bass Strait, and Port Phillip, the great bay on which, years later, the town of Melbourne was to grow.[1]

Baudin, though an experienced merchant service officer, was unfitted to be the leader of an exploring expedition; by his mismanagement and his neglect of the rules of naval hygiene made classic by Cook, disease and starvation had stricken both his ships, separating them in the wintry seas off the southern coasts and driving them, separately and unknown to each other, to seek the help of their country's enemies at the settlement of Port Jackson. When the *Géographe* reached the entrance to Sydney Harbour, her crew, 'in the last stages of scurvy and dysentery', had not the strength to sail her in; the ship lay helpless before the eyes of the man at the look-out on South Head until Governor King sent a boat-load of Flinders's men from the *Investigator* to bring her in.[2]

When the *Naturaliste*, the first of the French ships, arrived, news of the Peace of Amiens had not yet reached Sydney, but King's welcome was sincere and practical. A hundred and seventy Frenchmen were supplied from the low stocks of wheat by cutting down the residents' ration, King setting the example by reducing his own. The worst cases were taken to the hospital and everything possible was done to make them 'forget the hardships of a long and painful voyage'.

'Whatever the duties of hospitality may be', wrote Baudin, who though no hardy mariner was certainly a man of charm,

---

[1] Murray named the bay Port King, and King himself changed it to honour the name of Governor Phillip.

[2] *Terre Napoléon*, Ernest Scott.

'Governor King has given the whole of Europe the example of a benevolence which should be known, and which I take pleasure in publishing'. This was said in an open letter to Decaen, the Governor of the Isle-de-France, and was intended to secure the same hospitality for some unspecified British officer who might have need of it. But when Flinders was forced to put into the Isle-de-France with his ship in a leaking condition, he was detained by Decaen as a prisoner of war. It is a tragic story. The detention lasted more than six years; when at length he reached England he was a sick man, and he died after less than four years with the wife whom he had renounced for the voyage of discovery. What a waste of one of the ablest sea explorers the world has known! For Flinders, as a chartmaker, stands with Cook, and their work is the basis of all charts used in modern navigation on the Australian coast.

In the seven months that Baudin spent at Port Jackson, he received from the Governor far more than green vegetables, new anchors, and red wine. King and Chapman could both speak French well; Baudin and his officers were constantly at Government House. Surely it is not guessing to say that in Mrs. King's parlour, over her blue sprig teacups bought of Josiah Spode,[1] the conversation must often have turned to that other French explorer, the 'circumnavigator Mons. Peyrouse'. When Lapérouse had sailed into Botany Bay, all those years ago, just as the First Fleet under Phillip was giving up that harbour and moving to Port Jackson, Lieut. King of the *Sirius* with his knowledge of French had been chosen to board the Frenchman's vessel. Later, in the ship's cutter, he had been rowed all the way round from Port Jackson to Botany Bay and had spent the night aboard examining their charts, hearing what had been done and

[1] *King Papers*, 139–41.

what was planned. He had seen Cook's chart of Botany Bay lying before Lapérouse on the binnacle,[1] and to King had Lapérouse said 'Captain Cook has left me nothing to do but admire his achievements.'[2] King was the man, of all others, who could describe to these other Frenchmen how Lapérouse had looked and spoken just before he sailed into the blue, never to be seen again. No wonder that Baudin found King congenial and declared his intention of continuing the friendship by letter. And to Madame King he sent the most graceful letter, with a letterhead of an artistry surely unique among ship's notepaper, enclosing fifty English pounds to be distributed for the assistance of the orphans whose welfare was so dear to her heart.

And now there was a sequel to this so charming good-bye —a comical sequel with important results.

Immediately after they had gone, King was informed that it had been common talk among the Frenchmen that they were going to set up the French flag in Van Diemen's Land. King was in a quandary: Baudin and he had been on such confidential terms that he was certain that it was only gossip, and yet——He decided to send a small colonial vessel after Baudin with a midshipman to plant the flag of Britain 'just in case'. The midshipman found Baudin at King Island, delivered King's diplomatically worded letter, and proceeded agressively to plant His Majesty's colours right on top of the Frenchmen's tents. Baudin's short official reply disclaimed any knowledge of French plans of settlement; in his longer personal one, he gave the simple British sailor a piece of his philosophical French mind on the general subject of the justice of Europeans who 'seize in the name

---

[1] *Account of the Colony of New South Wales*, p. 5.

[2] 'Enfin, Monsieur Cook a tant fait qu'il ne m'a rien laissé à faire que d'admirer ses œuvres'. *Historical Records, N.S.W.* ii. 46.

of their Governments a land seen for the first time'. The inhabitants of such Islands, he said, sometimes unjustly labelled savages or cannibals, were but children of nature and actually no more uncivilized than 'your Scotch Highlanders or our peasants in Brittany' who, if they did not eat their fellow men, were just as objectionable. 'I have no knowledge', he wrote, 'of the claims which the French Government may have upon Van Diemen's Land, nor of its designs for the future; but I think that its title will not be any better grounded than yours. Everyone knows that Tasman and his heirs did not bequeath it by will to you.' As to the flag-hoisting episode, he was frankly displeased— a childish ceremony that was the more ridiculous from the flag's being placed upside down. A certain colleague with a witty pencil had made a clever caricature of the whole thing. Baudin had torn it up—but he evidently relished mentioning it. He ends with nice messages to Mrs. King and Mademoiselle Elizabeth, and many other friends. He dates his letter from King Island, which, he slily adds, 'I still call after you'.

One more friendly letter was written to King from the Isle-de-France; long before it reached him he had lost a friend, for Baudin was dead.

Afterwards, Governor and Mrs. King received from France a dessert service of Sèvres china, a recognition of the hospitality that they had shown to a foreign expedition in distress.[1]

As for the settlement of Van Diemen's Land, that was begun by establishing the post under Paterson on the north coast of the island; Port Phillip, the large harbour on the opposite shores of Bass Straits, King called 'a great acquisition' and regretted that he had nobody in Sydney equal to

[1] *Journal of Mme. de Falbe*, MSS.

the charge of making a settlement there. To make this settlement, Captain David Collins was sent from England in 1803 and landed his three hundred convicts on the harbour's sandy inner shore. Collins made no real effort to succeed; after three months he moved the establishment to Van Diemen's Land, founding Hobart in the south, and thus Melbourne's beginning was delayed for thirty-three years.

In those early days on Norfolk Island, King had been a devoted collector of specimens for Sir Joseph Banks. Now, in Sydney, overworked as he was and without a private secretary for much of the time, he never failed to keep Banks posted in the affairs of the Colony or to dispatch to him the plants and animals wanted for the great man's own collection or as an 'elegant addition' to the Royal one at Kew. Captains of vessels took charge of Government House gifts of waratahs and seedlings of Norfolk Island pines; cabins were loud with caged birds; baggage-rooms held boxes of samples of flax, specimens of improved fleeces, fragments of the new-found coal; and sometimes, 'tween decks, tribute to Banks or to King George, languished live kangaroos, emus, and black swans. Once King sent Banks an aboriginal's head, and the 'New Hollander' caused a sensation when the case was opened at the Customs House.

There was another specimen of even greater scientific interest that King dispatched to Sir Joseph soon after arriving in the Colony. In 1799, while King was still in England, somebody in New South Wales (possibly Governor Hunter) had sent Banks a drawing of a strange animal which he forwarded for identification to King, then on board the *Porpoise* with his family awaiting orders to sail. A number of people at Spithead, including ex-Governor Phillip and

Colonel Paterson, who was then on leave, examined the drawing and all agreed that 'no such creature was ever seen'. Cayley the botanist was told 'to keep a good look out for it' and promised to do his best 'to prove whether it is a deception or not'.[1] This was the first evidence to reach England of the existence of an animal that European scientists could not accept as true. When King reached New South Wales he found that the unbelievable animal did in fact exist. In 1800 he dispatched by Captain Kent in the *Buffalo* the 'water-mole', or 'duck-bill', which Banks desired, preserved in a keg of spirits.

This pickled platypus was probably the first of its kind to reach England and was one of the two specimens described under the name of *Ornithorhynchus Paradoxus* to the incredulous Royal Society by Everard Home in 1801, when ex-Governor Hunter, who was present at the meeting, was able to assure members that he had seen such animals with his own eyes.[2]

Throughout all these strenuous years King's health continued to trouble him, and though in 1803 he wrote valiantly that he was never too ill to do his duty, returning after each attack 'fresh to the charge', gout and the opposition of the military clique at last forced him to ask to be relieved of his post. In any case the understanding when he left England had been that he should return in five years.

As King himself was to write later, commenting on the reports that reached him in London of Sydney's growing restiveness under his successor, Bligh, there was no society where the clashing of duty and interest between the Governor

[1] *Historical Records, N.S.W.* iii. 679, 681.
[2] *Account of the English Colony of New South Wales. Philosophical Transactions of the Royal Society of London,* 1802, pt. I.
Historical Records, N.S.W. iv. 205 and 427. *The Platypus*; H. Burrell.

and the governed was more violent than in New South Wales, and more particularly so if the Governor did his duty. The hostility of the New South Wales Corps to a naval governor was in large part responsible for that clashing. King might and did have the approbation of successive ministers of State, and of King George, but in the Colony itself he continued to be in and out of hot water with the officers of the settlement, and Mrs. King, repeating history, often took a dip after him.

It was Macarthur, the Corps' most jealous officer, who in 1803 had asserted that if King were a man's enemy there could not be a stronger inducement to make Macarthur that man's friend.[1] It says much for the character and kindness of both the Kings that in 1805, by which time Macarthur was certainly more sheep-farmer than soldier, not only 'Mrs. Macarthur and the two girls' stayed at Government House for five weeks or more, but were joined there by Macarthur himself. 'I am happy to say', he wrote, 'that not a trace of former misunderstanding is now discoverable. Indeed, the Governor is uncommonly kind and obliging, and insomuch that I give you my word I am not very anxious for an immediate change.'[2]

However, the change was settled; Captain Bligh was daily expected to arrive.

The Kings' departure was almost as uncomfortable as their arrival—almost, but not quite. Doubtless with vivid memories of how they themselves had felt when taking over from a reluctant Hunter, they hastened to show Bligh all marks of respect and intended to board H.M.S. *Buffalo* within a week. But alas! King was ruled by gout to the end. He became seriously ill; departure was postponed and

---

[1] *Piper Correspondence*, iii. 469.
[2] Ibid. 473.

then still further delayed by the loss of grain in the Hawkesbury River floods and the possibility that the *Buffalo* would have to fetch food-supplies from the Cape. King did, however, relinquish the command of the Colony to Bligh, and retired to Government House at Parramatta, where from his bed he dictated informative letters to the new Governor. There was no William Chapman to act as his amanuensis; the letters are in the hand of his wife.[1] Tradition has it that Mrs. King had a great influence over her husband and was nicknamed Queen Josepha; certainly in one of those letters King refers to her as 'my under-secretary'—two proofs that she was no mere cipher in her husband's public life.

From an allusion in a postscript over 'the under-secretary's' own signature we learn of the existence of another little daughter, Mary, born at Government House in February 1805, the year of the Battle of Trafalgar; so that when the Kings finally went aboard H.M.S. *Buffalo* in February 1807, they were a family party of four.

As the people of Sydney watched the *Buffalo* work down to the Heads, it is doubtful if many of them realized what a good man they had lost. If King was not a man of great force he had three qualities of immeasurable importance; he was humane, he was just, and he was honest. He had shown all the industry, activity, and perseverance for which Governor Phillip had singled him out long ago; his merit, Banks now told him, had been great and his conduct deserving of much reward.

It was not then the custom to recognize the part played by wives of public servants in making or marring their husbands' work—in all the printed records there are no fanfares for Mrs. King; but when we do catch informal glimpses of her we see a cheerful, hard-working, generous-minded

[1] Mitchell Library MSS.

woman, with the enterprise and sense of fun that are essential in a successful pioneer. She was truly, as she was later to describe herself, her husband's partner in his labour and anxieties in the colony.

New South Wales, quite by chance, had been fortunate in its first Governor's wife.

CHAPTER VII

Exiled in England: Australia at last
1807-1844

THEY gave a farewell dinner-party on board while the ship still lay in the harbour, and the day they left a number of their friends accompanied them in boats three miles outside the Heads—amongst the friends their former enemy John Macarthur and his son Edward.[1] A squall approached and it became unsafe for the shore boats to come any farther; the last farewells were said. Mrs. King confessed in her ship's diary that from some of them she felt the parting very much.[2] She had hoped, too, to be able to call on the way home to say good-bye to her old friends on Norfolk Island—'I really long', she said, 'to see my old dwelling once more.'[3] King himself had wanted 'to attempt the Western passage through Bass's Straits, and to touch at the Cape of Good Hope'; neither wish was realized, for the *Buffalo* sailed via the coasts of New Zealand and Cape Horn.

Among the other passengers were the Marsdens, on their way to England to rouse interest in New Zealand as a mission-field and to secure preachers and teachers for New South Wales; and Lieut. Short of the Navy who, with his wife, six children, and a stock of farming implements, had sailed from home at the same time as Governor Bligh with the intention of settling in the colony and was already, the first victim of Bligh's despotism, returning to England under arrest.

The *Buffalo* made the Horn in nine weeks from Port

[1] Afterwards General Sir Edward Macarthur.
[2] *Buffalo* Diary.
[3] *Piper Correspondence*, i. 359.

95

Jackson—Mrs. King somewhat acidly comments that it was supposed to be a very fine passage—and another five weeks brought them to Rio Harbour. The 'fine passage' had its usual experience of gales, when mountainous seas smashed into the living-quarters, filling the ailing Mrs. Marsden's cot with water, soaking the convalescent Governor as he lay upon the sofa, ruining the plants, setting adrift the cage of birds that they were taking home for Governor Bligh, and drowning Mrs. King's 'poor little favorite bird'. There was a fire-ball that Mrs. King saw land on the quarter-deck with a flash and a bang, knocking over four men and disappearing down the main hatchway—there, they all expected, to make a hole in the bottom of the ship. For twenty minutes the pumps were constantly sounded and the ship's company held their breath: but the ball had mysteriously vanished. 'Where it made its escape, God only knows!' exclaims the diary.

For Mrs. King there was the constant duty of ministering to the sick, from her husband, who fell off the larboard ladder and sprained both wrists, to her cow, who refused to eat until given a warm mash of oatmeal and porter, which the cow 'relished'. Worst disaster of all was the death of poor Mrs. Short as they neared the snow-covered lands of Cape Horn; and most gruesome were the consequences of her dying request to her husband that her body be preserved and carried to England. There were no spirits in the ship and

'the only way', says Mrs. King, 'was to put her in a cask of pickle . . . had she reflected before her Death what was really necessary to be Done for the safety of all our Healths—I am sure poor Soul she would much rather have concented to a Watery Grave. Should it please God to take my Life on the Seas I shall not care what becomes of my Body provided it goes all together—

but to be mangled (as Poor Soul she was Done) is enough to frighten any Christian from Consenting to be served so—what consequences what becomes of the Body. The Soul, is the Grand and only concern. Poor Capt. Short is left with 6 Children to bemoan the loss of his Dear Wife—the youngest child is about 12 months old.'

A fortnight later the unfortunate little eldest daughter of this brood was included by the sympathetic Mrs. King in a dinner-party for the Governor's birthday. Afterwards they all danced reels and sang, and for the first time for seven years the Governor himself was well enough to join in the fun.

As they got into more northerly latitudes, they were coming to those seas off the South American coast where they might expect to meet the ships of Mrs. King's old enemy, Napoleon Bonaparte. On May 5th

'at ½ past Eleven at Night a sail was Discovered—we wore and observed she was coming towards us. She appeared a large Ship. . . . The appearance of this great ship put us all to the rout. The Women and children were all ordered to the Breadroom, where to my great concern I was obliged to go, with my young ones. On my entering the place a great Rat saluted me—which by the bye frighted me more than the fear of coming to action—never did I experience such a heat and had we not been released by the Commanding Officer I think I must have fainted with fright and fear—When she came quite near us Captain Houston hailed her which was not answered the first time When she was close alongside she answered and said she was the *Thisbe* Frigate 28 guns—Captain Sheppard going to the River Plat. She is taking out Forces under the Command of General Whitlock and General Gower to take the place in case it was not already in our possession.[1] As soon as each ship understood each other, the

[1] Lieut.-General John Whitelocke and Major-General John Leveson-Gower. The attack on Buenos Aires was a disastrous failure and Whitelocke was court-martialled and cashiered. *Dic. Nat. Biog.*

officers of the *Thisbe* came on board the *Buffalo*—They brought us a few English Newspapers—after exchanging the Latitude etc the officers returned to their ship—Captain Sheppard waited on the Governor at an early hour next morning. He took breakfast and then returned to the *Thisby*. The Governor returned with Captain Sheppard to pay his respects to Major-General Whitlock that gentleman felt our situation extremely... he was so good to send me 4 or 5 pounds of nice gingerbread, 2 pounds of tea and a very fine leg of English mutton, 21 bottles of Sodar water. As the Governor was going down the Side of the *Buffalo* he gave a jump down into the Boat and unfortunately sprained his foot which brought on the gout. In the evening the *Thisby* cheered us, which was returned by the *Buffalo* and we parted company.'

And, sad to say, the leg of mutton went bad.

By now the stocks of food and water were running low, they were delayed by head winds, and the Governor became very uneasy. The *Buffalo* was swarming with rats and leaking badly. One calm morning the ship trembled, there was a resounding crash, and the fore top-mast and yards carried away. 'I pray God', says Mrs. King 'that we may soon have a fair wind—god only knows what will become of [us] the ship is in a very bad State Increasing the Leaks and the Rigging Dreadfully bad—a something is gone every puff of wind.'

For Mrs. King, as well as the management of a mess on starvation rations, there was always, and increasingly, the care of a sick husband. The gaiety of the birthday-party was gone—gout ruled once more. The surgeon, Mr. McMillan, prescribed two pills: within a few hours of taking them the pains of gout were exchanged for symptoms of acute poisoning. His head swelled to a great size; he could not speak for a week or swallow food for nine days, and in any case Mrs. King had nothing fit to give him.

'Tripe and salt fish are the only things we have got to eat except a Pudding or Tart for the children. We are quite out of tea—the rats destroyed the greater part of 11 Flitches of Bacon and 9 Hams. . . . I really am quite Distressed what with managing our large Mess and my great anxiety about King—never was creature more distressed than I feel. . . .'

Becalmed a hundred and seventy miles from Rio, with less than a week's half-rations on board and King still dangerously ill, they welcomed gifts of some fowls and twenty oranges from a small coastal craft. Off the harbour's mouth, after the First Lieutenant, Oxley, had gone off in the cutter to request the pilot, there was a last storm—one of the worst nights of the voyage, the ship 'being quite embayed with the small islands'. Two days later, Mrs. King says that the ship has arrived off Rio, and the rest of the diary's pages are blank. Life had indeed become too full for even the anxious brevities of her journal.

In August, repaired and provisioned, they set sail once more. It was not long before the ship was leaking as badly as ever, but at last, on Sunday, November 8th, she came to a thankful anchor at Spithead.[1] The passengers scattered, as passengers do; Mr. Marsden to preach on the heathen state of New Zealand and to expound the possibilities of Australian wool; Lieut. Short, who on the voyage had lost a child as well as his wife, to face the court martial that was to acquit him with honour; and the Kings to be happily re-united at last to their son Phillip and to Maria, their 'darling girl'.

Their happiness was shortlived. After all the trials of the voyage King had arrived in England in good health, but since then, as Banks wrote to Bligh, he had been 'horribly

[1] Vide *The Memoirs of James Hardy Vaux* (London, 1819), a young convict who acted as amanuensis to King on board the vessel.

maul'd by the gout'. By now, King must have realized that although he was only forty-nine years old his days of activity were done. And if he could no longer work, what was he going to do to keep his wife and family? His pay as Governor, a thousand pounds a year, had ceased two years before on the day that he had handed the Colony over to Bligh—whose salary, incidentally, was double that of King's.[1] Now, all that King had to support his wife and six children was his half-pay as a Captain in the Navy and the interest on some small savings, a total of £220 a year. He had 'served His Majesty on sea and land nigh on forty years': beset with anxiety he now appealed to the King's bounty for his 'future provision and support'. For months he waited for a reply.

There is only one more glimpse of King. In September 1808 he paid a visit to his old friend Admiral Phillip at Bath —the man to whom King owed both the posts he had held in New South Wales. Phillip was crippled, King was frail, but the reunion must have heartened them both. King wrote of it to his son Phillip and hoped the letter would reach him before the boy departed on a Channel cruise.[2] Though neither knew it, the letter was probably King's farewell: he returned from Bath to London and a week later he was dead.

There can be little doubt that, had King lived, a pension would have been granted to him, as it had been to ex-Governors Phillip and Hunter. King had served in New South Wales throughout the twenty years of the Colony's existence and had established the three subordinate settlements of Newcastle, Port Dalrymple, and Hobart

---

[1] While in New South Wales, as well as his salary as Governor he had drawn full pay as principal commander of one of H.M.'s colonial ships— a welcome addition to his 'shattered means'.

[2] *Naval Pioneers of Australia*, 166.

Town; at the end of the period he had been relieved at his own request and had received His Majesty's 'entire approbation' of his conduct of 'the important charge'. Phillip's annual pension was £500, Hunter's £300. Hunter's service was much less arduous than Phillip's and much shorter than King's, and ended, justly or unjustly, with official censure and his recall. King's pension would scarcely have been less than Hunter's.

But the mills of the Treasury grind slowly. King's appeal was written in May; by September, when he died, no action had been taken and he died with the dark cloud of his anxiety undispelled.

Poor Mrs. King, left a widow at forty-three, was at first in great financial straits. She had to support her son and three young daughters and apparently also her husband's mother. Did she attempt still to help Norfolk and Sydney,[1] or was she obliged after this to let them fend for themselves? No wonder if, with all these responsibilities, she was at her wits' end.

Just before he died, King had written again to the Secretary of State, Viscount Castlereagh, reminding him with pathetic urgency of the lamentable state of his affairs. Evidently, in the confused days of his last illness, the letter was not sent. It reached Castlereagh some months later when Mrs. King, searching for help, enclosed it to him in a letter of her own. At length her petition bore fruit and a life annuity of £200 was granted to her as a matter of grace. In reality the sum was smaller, because the receipt of this allowance, as Mrs. King vainly pointed out to Banks and other influential friends, deprived her of her right to a widow's pension of £80. The mills of the Treasury had ground exceeding small.

[1] Cf. Appendix I.

EXILED IN ENGLAND: AUSTRALIA AT LAST

The Macarthurs' young son, Edward, to whom the Kings had waved good-bye from the deck of the *Buffalo* outside the Sydney Heads, had arrived in England carrying dispatches telling of the arrest of Governor Bligh. In London he saw something of Mrs. King and wrote to his people that she was in great distress of mind about her 'disunited' affairs. 'The contrast', he said, 'of her present situation with that she has possessed makes her very unhappy.'

Her present situation was indeed bad; but at the other end of the world were some assets that gave to her future a gleam of hope. These were some acres of land near Parramatta—seven hundred and ninety of her own and smaller areas belonging to each of her children. Grazing on those lands were some hundred head of cattle. Mrs. King's title to these animals was doubtful, but it was they that were to bring her prosperity in after years.[1]

Already in 1810 Marsden, who looked after Mrs. King's colonial interests, assured her that her concern was now very great and needed much care; a few years later, actual prosperity was hers. An atmosphere of general well-being is breathed from some of her gossipy letters dated round about the Battle of Waterloo, and written from England to her old friend Captain Piper in Sydney.[2] Her dear Maria, returned to Sydney some time since as the wife of John Macarthur's nephew, Hannibal Hawkins Macarthur, has written to Mrs. King announcing the birth of her baby, and Mrs. King learns that Governor Macquarie has been so kind as to give Maria some land; Phillip is expected home from the Mediterranean and is bent upon going to New South Wales; she hopes on Thursday to be able to take Elizabeth to the Upper Rooms, as she has subscribed to the Balls

[1] See Appendix II.
[2] *Piper Correspondence*, iii. 363, 369.

(did their skirts brush those of the immortal Jane?). She fancies that at Sydney they are 'all very gay at this time at the Government House dancing away' and hopes to be favoured with 'a long account of every particular'. To Captain Piper she announces 'the glorious termination of war', after Napoleon's retirement to Elba.

'How wonderful Providence has ordained all things', she ejaculates in a breathless crescendo of satisfaction, 'to occasion the Wretch who has sacrificed the lives of millions to agrandize himself to defeat his own intentions for he might at this moment have been an Emperor with large dominions had he not by grasping at more, lost *all and himself Dethroned* and Exiled *himself* I always thought that Scourge of mankind Bunoaparte [sic] would be crushed at last.'

A few months later,

'everybody is going to France—I should be most happy to go—provided we had a gentleman to go with me. . . . We have a peace, but as yet we do not feel it. Everything but bread is as high priced as when you were in England, the income tax is not taken off, it is said we must not expect that it will be taken off, I fear the public will not like it.'

Europe, indeed, exists and is important; but one feels that her heart is in New South Wales. It is not only Phillip who is bent upon going there: she yearns to go too. It was there that her husband, dying in London, had wished he could end his days, and at his death and ever since, Mrs. King had longed to get back herself. But now she hears strange things of the Colony—at her time of life she must confess she would not like to be made uncomfortable, though she thinks it very much depends upon ourselves the being so or not. And Maria, sad to say, appears to have a great dislike to her going out to New South Wales. 'I should have thought,' says Mrs. King wistfully, 'I should have thought she would have been pleased to have me near her.' It gives her 'a sort of wavering'. She longs for letters, thirsts for news. 'The letters I did receive were *very, very* short—not a word of the new discovered country across the mountains and many other things which would have interested me extremely.'

It was not only Maria who opposed her return. 'Everybody persuades my not going out', she wrote, 'but I shall take my son's opinion.' She awaits impatiently his arrival from the Mediterranean, for 'my son's return will determine all my future plans'. Meantime she gives directions for the building of a house in Sydney on land granted her by Governor Macquarie, and asks for the sizes of the windows so that she may send out the glass. But alas! Phillip's vote must have been against her going: when he sailed for New South Wales in 1817 to carry out a coastal survey he took with him, not his mother, but a young wife.

A long fifteen years were to pass before Mrs. King got the wish of her heart. Mary, the youngest daughter, had followed Maria and was settled in New South Wales with Robert Lethbridge, her Cornish husband; Elizabeth, after a broken engagement, was safely married to a widower, Charles Runciman, a London artist of some standing;[1] and now, in 1832, after a period of distinguished scientific naval service, Phillip was to return for good to his colonial home. She would go with him. No more would she live in the past, gathering what warmth she could from recollection, consorting whenever possible with visitors to London from New South Wales, with ex-officials of the Colony or their widows taking the waters at Bath. Those days were over— she returned to Sydney to live in the present.

Her ship's arrival was signalled, not by flags from

[1] *Memoirs of P. G. King the Younger.*

EXILED IN ENGLAND: AUSTRALIA AT LAST

Governor Phillip's mast as the *Gorgon* was in 1791, but by 'a Telegraphic Light from South Head' that enabled her son-in-law Hannibal Macarthur at Parramatta to be in Sydney 'with suitable conveyances to remove Mrs. King and family before the ship anchored in the Cove'.[1] She was a grandmother, with ringlets and crinoline, but 'so very little changed', writes her old friend Mrs. Macarthur of Camden Park, and 'as gay as ever'. Once more she was under the same roof as people who were making history. Her son, front-rank hydrographer and commander of the *Adventure* and *Beagle* survey expedition, had been elected a Fellow of the Royal Society for his work in charting the coasts that Flinders had first explored; a grandson was one of the two who first penetrated the south-eastern portion of the Colony and named it Gippsland after Governor Gipps; she saw the spread of the pastoralists inland beyond the Blue Mountains that in her husband's day had confined the settlement to the arid edge; she lived in the thick of the disputes and ardours of the Colony's development from a prison house to a free community with a measure of self-government. She had three married children close beside her, and twenty-six grandchildren to give her a strong personal interest in the Colony's future.

Her last eight years were spent under the roof of her eldest daughter, the once lovely Maria, now an invalid. It was Maria's youngest daughter, Emmeline, who, when she herself was old and in possession of the Sèvres dessert service of Baudin fame, jotted down some recollections that give us a last picture of Mrs. King.[2]

Emmeline describes her parents' old home, The Vineyard, on the Parramatta River and its enlargement from the

[1] Unpublished letters of Elizabeth Macarthur. The ship was *The Brothers*.
[2] Unpublished journal of Mme Vigant de Falbe.

original cottage to a lovely house finished in 1836.[1] It was her grandmother, Mrs. King, who, to the child's wonder, put real money under the foundation stone—a handsome, tall, and stately grandmother 'with beautiful hair dressed high under a tulle cap, and a row of sausage-shaped curls of false hair in front à la mode'. Her son built a stable for her use and she had her own carriage and pair, coachman, boy, and maid. The children were taught to reverence her; she always sat at her son-in-law's right hand at family prayers. She used to give the children money as birthday presents, 'commencing at five shillings and gradually increasing till the joyful day when an order for £1 was the gift'. 'I can see her now', says the writer, 'always handsomely dressed and generally wearing an embroidered apron, and some white lace or embroidery on her shoulders. Quite a picture', she adds.

Not only a picture, but quite evidently an influence in that patriarchal establishment with its gardens, orange grove, and vineyard set between the curve of the Parramatta River and the forest of native trees; with its active master, the adored invalid mistress, its troop of 'radiantly happy' children; its Scottish maids and English free men for indoor staff, its numerous convict servants for out-door work who were never allowed to cross the threshold of the home. The house was never without visitors; no day was dull. There were picnics on the river, and gay weddings that grew from the picnics, and jam-making parties that were as merry as the marriages; Twelfth Night celebrations got up by Grandmother King to amuse the children and the neighbours; constant visits from the Macarthur cousins at Camden and the seven sons of Phillip King at Dunheved across the river.

[1] Now the Subiaco Convent.

EXILED IN ENGLAND: AUSTRALIA AT LAST

Sunday at the Vineyard had its ritual, and everybody was expected to go to church. Some of the party drove the three miles to St. John's, Parramatta, in 'the britska' that held five; a favoured child—and it was usually Emmeline—would be honoured with the little seat drawn out in the middle of Mrs. King's own carriage; the overflow rowed up the river or walked across the fields. The church was bare, the pews were enclosed, the sermons were long: the preacher, the same Samuel Marsden who had exhorted the Kings and Sydney's store-house congregation in the year eighteen hundred and one.

On Sunday afternoon 'all the world went for a walk and in the evening Papa read a short sermon and the children suffered fidgets'. On the walls, looking down on the goodly congregation, were the portraits of George III and his Queen in their coronation robes. These had been presented by His Majesty to King in his capacity as Governor when he came out to New South Wales, and they had hung in the long drawing-room at Government House. The Kings evidently regarded them as private property, for when they returned to England the pictures went too. For years the life-sized portraits in their heavy gilt frames had ennobled the walls of Mrs. King's London house in Edgware Road, dazzling the young Australian grandsons who made it their home in the school holidays; the portraits had returned with Mrs. King to New South Wales, and now in the reign of Queen Victoria it was little Emmeline and her brothers and sisters who delighted in the red and the ermine, and especially in the garter round the Royal Leg. Later, somebody in authority put the view that the pictures had never been intended as a private gift; Mrs. King held to her opinion but compromised gracefully by presenting them to the Government before her death, and they hang in Government House, Sydney, at the present day.[1]

Mrs. King was no mere Sunday-Christian: she was still known for the goodness that young Chapman had so warmly praised, and on week-days was to be met driving about the country-side, taking help to the sick and suffering, as she had always loved to do. She even had the hardihood to vaccinate the local children,[2] being familiar with the practice since the days when Surgeon John Savage, disciple of Jenner, had 'introduced the cow-pock' to the Colony in 1803.

The days of convict servants, such as were to be found at the Vineyard, on the Dunheved estate, at Camden and elsewhere, were numbered. Mrs. King was to live to see the abolition of transportation, the system that had caused her own migration to the ends of the earth. Close to the Vineyard, that prosperous and happy home, was a reminder of the sinister origin of the Colony's existence, the local prison-barracks. From behind their bars, the convicts used to watch the care-free Macarthurs embarking at the jetty in their boat on some pleasure bent, never suspecting that amongst the picknickers was at least one, the gentle Emmeline, for whom the sight of the prison-faces cast a shadow on the day. Soon, no more convicts were to be met, yellow-clad and in irons, marching to their labours under guard. The prison was turned into military barracks and the Sunday procession from the Vineyard went to church to the music of the regimental band. Emmeline was happy and the colony was one big step nearer to maturity.

[1] P. G. King the younger states that the portraits are the work of Sir Thomas Lawrence, but there appears to be no historical or artistic basis for this claim.
[2] William Freame, newspaper article, Mitchell Library.

There was one memorable day in 1840 when the family was gathered at dinner to celebrate some anniversary. Grandmother King was there, and even the young ones were allowed to come to the table; but there was one important absentee. This was James, the eldest son of the house, who had not returned from an exploring expedition to the southeast with the Polish scientist Count Strzelecki. Great anxiety was felt for their fate in the heavily timbered mountains of that wild country; joy was unbounded when James arrived unexpectedly in the middle of dinner and made the circle complete. What tales he must have told that night of the adventure that had so nearly ended in death! Only the bush-craft and devotion of James's aboriginal servant, Charlie Tara, had saved the party from perishing in the dense scrub. Owing to him, James was once more safe at home and Maria Macarthur able to record in her diary a prayer of thanksgiving for her son's return.

Next morning some of the family left the Vineyard; the circle was broken, never to be complete again.

Mrs. King, the 'stately old grandmother' to whom they were all devoted, was also to leave them soon, and for ever. There came a day when Mrs. John Macarthur, in her faithful chronicle to her soldier son Edward, reported that Mrs. King, so often a visitor to Camden and always full of inquiries for Edward's news, was 'rather in a declining way'; a few weeks later the chronicle told him of Mrs. King's death, in her eightieth year.[1] Maria was too ill to be with her mother; it was the sixteen-year-old Emmeline who held her hand at the end. She was buried in the graveyard of St. Mary's, South Creek, near Parramatta—the little church built in her life-time on land given by her son to fulfil his mother's great wish.

[1] She died on July 26th, 1844.

EXILED IN ENGLAND: AUSTRALIA AT LAST

Sydney Smith once published in the *Edinburgh Review* an essay about Botany Bay, based on Collins's book on the earliest years of *The English Colony of New South Wales*. It evidently amused the somewhat condescending young philosopher to read 'the account of a whole nation exerting itself to new-floor the government house, repair the hospital, or build a wooden receptacle for stores'. In the future, he asks, when the Colony has reached a position of power and wealth (but one feels he thought the supposition fantastic) 'who will ever remember that the sawing of a few planks, and the knocking together of a few nails, were such a serious trial of the energies and resources of the nation?'

Anna Josepha King, the Governor's Lady of Norfolk Island and of Sydney, New South Wales, was one of those who helped to saw the planks and knock together the nails of the nation's earliest dwelling. It would be sad if those who live in the solid mansion that succeeds it were to forget altogether that she was amongst the faithful and courageous builders of the past.

MELBOURNE, 1938-9.

APPENDIX I

The Children of Governor King

THE children of Governor and Mrs. King were Phillip Parker (b. Norfolk Island, December 13th, 1791), Anna Maria (b. Norfolk Island, April 22nd, 1793), Utricia (b. Norfolk Island, 1795, ? October), Elizabeth (b. at sea on board East Indiaman *Contractor*, February 10th, 1797), and Mary (b. Sydney, February 1st, 1805).

Phillip (m. Harriet Lethbridge, 1817) had eight children; Maria (m. Hannibal Hawkins Macarthur, 1812) had eleven, and Mary (m. Robert Copland Lethbridge, 1826) had seven. The numerous Australian descendants of Governor King trace their connexion with him directly through one of these three, Phillip, Maria, or Mary. Elizabeth married a widower named Runciman, an artist, and apparently remained in England. Utricia died prior to August 1799.

Maria's marriage to a Macarthur joined two families that had often been bitterly opposed; Phillip's and Mary's strengthened an old association. While King was in Norfolk Island a former friend wrote to him from Cornwall to renew a broken intimacy. 'If this gets to your hands', he wrote, 'I shall hope to have an answer with an account of yourself and family who no doubt begin to be numerous and a young King born in Norfolk Island may perhaps some twenty years hence be ye husband of a Cornish wife.'[1] The writer was Christopher Lethbridge of Launceston. King kept the letter and the prophecy came true. Indeed, not only did Phillip marry Lethbridge's daughter Harriet in 1817, but in 1826 Lethbridge's son Robert married Mary King.

Phillip had a notable career. After ten years of active service he distinguished himself as a hydrographer in South American and Australian waters and was elected a Fellow of the Royal Society. In later life he was promoted to the rank of Rear-Admiral. In 1832 he settled on his colonial estate, Dunheved,

[1] *King Papers*, i. 127.

APPENDIX I

where he brought up his family of eight and devoted himself to farming and to political interests.

Governor King had two illegitimate sons. The elder, Norfolk, the first child born on Norfolk Island, was born on January 8th, 1789. The exact date and place of the birth of the second son, Sydney, has not been ascertained but was probably early in 1790 and must have been either on the Island or at Sydney itself; he could have been named after Sydney Bay, Norfolk Island, or after the parent settlement in New South Wales.

Who was their mother? Her name will not be found anywhere set beside Governor King's, but the tale can be pieced together from records, some already in print. It begins on the day after the First Fleet sailed into Port Jackson, while the convicts were still imprisoned on the transports and the Cove was still a place of undisturbed enchantment. The voyage, with its horrors of overcrowding, dirt and disease, was done; the squalor of the struggle on land had not begun. King already knew that he was to have no part in that struggle but was to leave almost at once with a small party to form a settlement on uninhabited Norfolk Island 'to prevent its being occupied by any other European power'. On that Sunday afternoon he went aboard the *Lady Penrhyn*, female convict transport, to consult Lieut. Bowes, the surgeon, 'respecting the characters of 5 or 6 women whom he meant to take with him'.

'He has made choice of such of both sexes whose characters stand fairest', says Bowes, 'and has held out such encouragements to them upon their behaving properly as must render their situation very comfortable; at the same time he assur'd them that he sh'd not undertake to punish them in case of misbehaviour there, as the greatest punishment he c'd inflict upon them he sh'd send them back to this place to be dealt with according to their demerits; he also assured them that they w'd not be hardwork'd, and w'd be convey'd home to England (if they chose it) at the expiration of their term of transportation, and perhaps, if they wish'd it, they w'd be sent home even before the expiration of it. He also informed them that it was the pleasure of the Governor [Phillip] if any of them had any person among the convicts who were going to whom they have an acquaintance, or if any partiallity sh'd take place between any 2 of them on their voyage to Norfolk

THE CHILDREN OF GOVERNOR KING

Island or after their arrival there, they had his permission to marry; that he had authorized the surgeon to perform that office, and after a time the clergyman would be sent there to remarry them.'

One of the six, despite these persuasive arguments, was unwilling to go, but for the other five the unknown island apparently held more promise than the cove in which they lay. A few days later the five were landed by themselves, and before any of the other women, in a place withdrawn from the turmoil of the main encampment, 'on the left side of the cove, near the Governor's house'. Their characters 'stood the fairest' and they were to be kept so. Another woman being found to complete the party, King sailed a week later for the Island with his little group of marines and convict men and the six women—a Sarah, an Olivia, three Elizabeths, and one Ann—Ann Inett, of Worcestershire;[1] and it was Ann who became the mother of King's two sons.

During his two years on 'ye isle' King kept a daily tabular journal of events of importance to the little community, noting the weather and such items as the amount of fish caught, persons sick or punished, and crops sown or cut. In the entry for Thursday, January 8th, after the routine note on the wind and state of the surf, King wrote '1 male child born'. Ten days later, on the Sunday—a clear morning with not the least surf—he says 'At 10 a.m. performed divine service, and baptized the new-born infant by the name of Norfolk, he being the first born on the island.' No hint here of his paternity, or of the emotions that must have been aroused by the event; no word, of course, of the mother: but King turned back the pages of his journal and in the margin opposite the laconic entry of January 8th he wrote in pencil the name 'Norfolk'.

What did King do with his two infant sons when he left the Island and Sydney in a starving condition in 1790 and set out via Batavia for England? Even in that age of disregard for infant welfare it is hardly credible that he would take them with him on a more than ordinarily hazardous voyage: and when Mrs. Parker, in her account of her *Voyage Round the World*, says that the Kings came aboard the *Gorgon* at Spithead with 'their family'

[1] *Pioneers of Sydney Cove*, p. 53.

I

APPENDIX I

she is almost certainly using the word loosely to denote attendants. The earliest Island record—The Norfolk Island Victualling List—shows that Ann had left before 1792, although her five companions were still there: the probability is that she was taken away by King when he left there himself and that she and the two children remained in Sydney during his absence in England. The List's later entries show that Norfolk (but not the younger boy) returned from Sydney to the Island with King when the Lieut.-Governor himself returned in 1791, bringing his wife. A year later, Ann married at Parramatta. Her husband had been transported for life: something of King's debt to Ann Inett may perhaps be considered as paid when he granted her husband an absolute pardon in January 1804.[1]

Letters show that Sydney, a delicate child, was in England in 1795, under the somewhat resentful care of his Grandmother King.[2] Norfolk went to England in 1796, leaving the Island just before the Governor and Mrs. King and their family, and travelling alone in the *Marquis Cornwallis*. William Chapman, official storekeeper on the Island and King's unofficial secretary and their friend and confidant, wrote to his mother:

'Norfolk goes home in the Cornwallis, you will therefore most likely see him in London, he is going down to Mrs. King's mother at Bideford, and as the Govr. does not wish any of his own relations to be troubled with him he begs you will not mention it to Mrs. King or indeed to anybody, as he wishes it to be kept a secret that he is sent home, if you should see him he will give you a very particular account of the Island, and every person on it, and particularly of me.'[3]

In 1799 both boys were in the care of a Mr. Chapman in Yorkshire, who educated them until they entered the Navy. In July of that year, when King was expecting momentarily to sail from England to New South Wales and was making final arrangements for Phillip and Maria, he wrote detailed directions to Chapman respecting 'the Two Boys' and their training in the three R's and in religion—the observance of which he trusts 'our

[1] Official records; information from Mr. T. D. Mutch, of Sydney.
[2] *King Papers*, i. 123, 169.
[3] *Chapman Papers*, letter June 8, 1796.

Youth will never forget notwithstanding the atheistical example of our neighbours'. To the boys themselves he wrote letters that show that they were not debarred from their share of family love and care.

'Dear Norfolk,
I am sorry it has been out of my power either to send for you to this place, or to go and see you, as I have not been able to go out of sight of the ship for the last 18 months, and it is only now that we have received orders ... when you get on board the *Rowcliffe* always say your prayers and do not forget your catechism and God will bless you and preserve you when you are fighting the French, never forget God Almighty and recollect that he sees all your actions. If you hear others swear do not do as they do, as they have never been taught better. ... I hope to have a very long letter from you the first opportunity after you are entered a Midshipman in His Majesty's Navy, which you must take care never to disgrace by being naughty while young or behaving ill when you are a man. Phillip and Elizabeth desire their kind love to you. Phillip is got to the end of subtraction, he is determined to be a sailor also. When you go to London you will go to a gentleman who will carry you to see Maria at Greenwich. Remember that you always love Sydney and think on all with that affection with which I am, dear Norfolk, affectionately,

Philip Gidley King.'

To Sydney he writes at the same time:

'You must write to Norfolk when he leaves you and always love him. You will write to me often and let me know what trade or profession you would like to be of, and I will do everything to make you a great man. You must make yourself a good man (which you must be to be a great man) by attending to Mr. Chapman's advice and instruction. Mrs. King, Phillip and Elizabeth all desire their loves to you, and hope you will always pray for them as they do for you....'[1]

There is extant a letter from Norfolk to Phillip written in a large copy-book hand, when he was still happily one of the family and unaware of the difficulties that beset the path of children of irregular parentage.

[1] *King Papers*, ii. 201–6.

APPENDIX I

'Lymington,
January 17th, 1801.

'Dear Brother,
I am with Admiral Phillip and have had the Measles but am now well and taking Physick and when the Rowclift comes from Jersey I am to go on bord. I hope you and Maria are both well and desire you will send my Love to her when you writ to her and when you see the Admiral who is coming to Town. I shall be glad if you will let me hear from you being with Love and esteem,
Dear Phillip
Yours most affectionately,
Norfolk King.
P.S. Mrs. Phillip desires her Love to you and Maria and the Admiral does the same.'[1]

In 1816, when Norfolk was a lieutenant and twenty-seven years old, his father and his father's friend, 'the Admiral', were dead. The wars were over: for Norfolk they had ended with a period of captivity in American hands.[2] Now without influence, he was anxious to return to the part of the world where he was born. He wrote to the Secretary of State, informing him that he was King's son and supposed to be the first human being born on Norfolk Island, where he held a grant of land. Settlement on the Island being now given up and the people moved to Van Diemen's Land, he asked to be given land there to compensate him for the loss of his Island grant. As a result, the Governor of New South Wales was directed to put Norfolk on the same footing as other ex-Island landowners; but Norfolk was informed that the Secretary of State could not grant his further request for 'his Lordship's interest' to enable him to get out to settle in Van Diemen's Land as free passages to the Colony were no longer given.

Norfolk's claim to be an Island landowner was correct—at the age of four he had received 50 acres there, a property called Norfolk Farm;[3] but the State Archives in Tasmania have no

[1] *King Papers*, ii. 249.
[2] Ingleton, *Charting a Continent*, p. 39, where a few details of Norfolk's naval career may be found.
[3] Register of New South Wales Lands Department: information from Mr. T. D. Mutch, of Sydney.

THE CHILDREN OF GOVERNOR KING

record of a compensatory grant in Van Diemen's Land and his name continued in the Navy Lists until his death in 1839. The Lists included Sydney, also a lieutenant, until he died in 1840. What sort of men they were, and how they spent their lives, is unknown.

APPENDIX II

The Kings, some Land, and the Wild Cattle

THAT land, and those cattle! Both possessions must have been discussed threadbare by the Kings, in the Colony and later in London when they were fighting his failing health and the nightmare of their finances.

The 790 acres were granted to Mrs. King by Governor Bligh in 1806 after King (who had himself never owned land) had granted 1,345 acres to Governor Bligh. The Editor of the Historical Records of Australia points[1] to the great irregularity of these transactions between governors, the suspicious nature of which is underlined by the name the official register gives to Bligh's grant to Mrs. King—'*Thanks!*' The same critic tells the story of an earlier attempt of King's to get for his family the security that his salary failed to give. In 1804 he had made a grant of over 2,000 acres to his wife, but this was cancelled before being issued, as it was illegal. In 1806, when King was expecting his successor, he made grants to Phillip (then fourteen years old), to Maria, and to Elizabeth and Mary; and these grants covered the same area as the one originally made out to Anna Josepha King. Although such an irregularity is impossible to defend, and is a little surprising in one of King's tender conscience, it should be remembered that at that time it may well have seemed harmless enough to earmark two thousand acres in an unexplored continent almost as big as Europe.

Amongst the miscellaneous stock landed with the first settlers in 1788 were a number of humped cattle from the Cape of Good Hope. At the end of the first few months of hardship for man and beast, the greatest part of the stock was dead and, as Governor Phillip sadly wrote, 'from the inattention of the men who had the cattle, those belonging to the Government and two cows belonging to myself are lost. As they have been missing three weeks it is probable they are killed by the natives. . . . The loss

[1] In Series I, iv, p. xvii, and v, p. x.

APPENDIX II

of four cows and two bulls falls very heavy.' Phillip always understated his troubles: the settlement was left with only a calf; the loss was worse than heavy—it was disastrous.

The precious little herd that Phillip thought were speared by blacks had in reality made off into the bush. Not until 1795 were they discovered with their progeny stamping and bellowing west of the Nepean River in an area of well-watered grazing ground unpenetrated till then. There were sixty of them—a rich addition to a Colony still very much in difficulties; but so fierce were they, and so far from Sydney—all of fifty miles—that they were potential wealth only. For some years they were intermittently heard and seen in the fine country that became known as the Cow Pastures. In the hot December of 1803, when the cattle numbered several hundreds, Governor King's party came to close quarters with them and only a timely thwack of King's riding-crop across the nose of a charging bull saved the Governor from being unhorsed. A little later the botanist Caley, exploring the 'interior', found a broad track beaten by their hooves into a highway so good that he called it the London Road. Official plans were made from time to time for the capture of the cattle, and occasionally the more intrepid and westerly settlers unofficially helped themselves; but still most of the wild herd roamed at liberty, increasing with every year.

In 1801 Phillip wrote from London to King giving him 'full power to take possession of, and dispose of, as your property, my claim on, and share in, the cattle running wild in the woods and two cows belonging to me, having strayed with the cows belonging to the Crown.' By 1804 the cattle still eluded capture. King wrote to London asking for permission to exchange his claim on Phillip's cattle for some out of the Government tame herds. He could not, he said, neglect taking advantage of the gift, as he had a large family, no savings, and no certainty of the duration of life. He reckoned the wild cattle to be now at least 5,000, but cut that guess down to 3,000, estimated his share as 1,300, and reduced his claim to a modest 300 head. In Downing Street, the matter must have seemed both trifling and far-fetched: one can see the Minister raising an amused eyebrow and letting the matter slide. Eighteen months later King wrote again, informing their Lordships that, as more important affairs must have prevented a reply to his request, he had made the proposed selection from the tame herds and caused the beasts to be pastured by themselves.

After her husband's death Mrs. King, uneasy as to her security, addressed a long letter to Viscount Castlereagh begging him to ratify the exchange formally. In this letter somebody had obviously helped her to round her periods, to express her natural worry in artificial phrases calculated to impress a Minister of State; but through the screen of gentility one can see the real harassed woman determined to make sure of the means of bringing up her children, to know whether she can count on the income from this source. Downing Street raised its eyebrows once more: damn those cows.

'Madam', wrote Castlereagh, 'I received your letter reviving a claim which was made by the late Governor King for some compensation for a few cattle, which escaped into the woods. . . . This claim when originally made was conceived by Government of so very loose a nature that it was not considered right to make any order upon the subject. I feel much regret in stating that after so long a period as has elapsed since the first escape of the cattle it is not possible to consider of compensation for a mere private loss, originating from neglect.'

Castlereagh neither permitted nor forbade: he left it in the air. It is not to be imagined for a moment that Mrs. King instructed her agent in New South Wales to hand the cattle back.

When Governor Macquarie, with his wife and the gentlemen of his household, went on a tour of inspection of 'the interior parts of the Colony' in 1810, they visited 'Mrs. King's Farm on the Right Bank of the South Creek'. There 'we halted for a short while to look at her fine numerous herds of horned cattle, of which she has upwards of 700 Head of all descriptions . . . we found them in a very high condition.'[1]

Evidently, it was not Ministers of State alone who could successfully let things slide.

The Wild Cattle remained a problem for years, monopolizing

[1] *Macquarie's Tour in New South Wales.*

APPENDIX II

'the best land on this side of the Blue Mountains' and encouraging the art of cattle-lifting among the nearest settlers and their servants, the employees of John Macarthur of Camden himself not being above suspicion.[1] Stealing the cattle was proclaimed a felony punishable by death, and military guards and constables were stationed for forty miles along the Nepean River, but such measures proved useless in controlling the depredations of 'all the idle and disorderly characters in the Colony'. At last the exasperated Governor Macquarie asked the Secretary of State to let him shoot the beasts and salt them down for the King's Stores, 'to free the country of the Banditti of Bush Rangers'. This was not done and settlement of the Cow Pastures was delayed until 1820. However, by 1822 the beasts were well on the way to amalgamation with the Government tame herds turned out on the Pastures, and thereafter the topic of the Wild Cattle dropped out of official dispatches.

So ended the story that began with two bulls, four cows, and one careless convict cowherd in 1788.

[1] Macarthur dismissed one of his men for stealing and killing calves from the Government herds. This man and another, dismissed from the Macarthur household for thieving, were amongst the 'infamous characters' on the staff of the Sydney gaol when Macarthur was imprisoned there, under arrest prior to the famous mutiny against Bligh in 1808.

APPENDIX III
Bibliography

1. PUBLISHED SOURCES.

   Phillip's Voyage to Botany Bay. 1790.
   Historical Journal of the Transactions of Port Jackson and Norfolk Island (including the journal of Lieut. King).
   Captain John Hunter, 1793.
   Historical Records of New South Wales, Vols. I–VII.
   Historical Records of Australia, Series I, Vols. I, IV, V, IX.
   The English Colony in New South Wales. Collins, 1803.
   Sydney Gazette and New South Wales Advertiser.
   Voyage around the World in the *Gorgon* Man of War. Mary Ann Parker, 1795.
   Voyage of H.M.S. *Pandora*. Edwards and Hamilton, 1790–1.
   Mémoires du Capitaine Péron sur ses Voyages.
   Phillip of Australia. M. Barnard Eldershaw.
   The Macarthurs of Camden. S. Macarthur Onslow.
   Pioneers of Sydney Cove. H. J. Rumsey.
   Life of Matthew Flinders. Ernest Scott.
   The Memoirs of James Hardy Vaux
   Terre Napoléon. Ernest Scott.
   Naval Pioneers of Australia. Becke & Jeffery.
   South Africa a Century Ago. W. H. Wilkins.
   The Australian Encyclopedia.
   Burke's Colonial Gentry.
   Dictionary of National Biography.
   Charting a Continent. Geoffrey C. Ingleton, Lieutenant-Commander, R.A.N. (ret.) 1944.

2. MANUSCRIPT SOURCES.

   (a) *In the Mitchell Library, Sydney.*
   Bowes' Journal 1787-8-9.
   Norfolk Island Victualling List, 1792–5.
   Journal of the Transactions on Norfolk Island, by P. G. King, 1788–90.

APPENDIX III

King Papers, Vols. I and II, Correspondence Vol. I.
Chapman Papers.
Banks Papers, Vols. XI and XVIII.
Piper Correspondence Vols. I and III.
Journal of Lieut. R. Clark, 1787–92.
Mrs. King's Diary of the Voyage to Australia on board the whaler *Speedy*, 1799.
Mrs. King's Diary of the Voyage to England on board H.M.S. *Buffalo*, 1807.
Macquarie's Tour in New South Wales, 1810.
Memoirs of P. G. King the Younger.
Letters of Elizabeth Macarthur, Camden Papers, in the possession of the Macarthur Onslow family, N.S.W.

(*b*) *Other Manuscript Sources.*

Journal of Mme Vigant de Falbe, copy in the possession of the Misses Macarthur King, Sydney.
Flinders Papers, Melbourne Public Library transcripts.

INDEX

Adventure, H.M.S., 330 tons, 105.
Africa, 82; *see also* South Africa.
Amiens, Peace of, 86.
Atlantic, store-ship, 223 tons, 20, 23.
Austen, Jane, 2, 7, 102.
Australia, 1, 53.

Balmain, William, Surgeon, 20, 30, 31, 64.
Banks, Sir Joseph, 3, 33–6, 38, 42, 68, 75, 77–8, 80, 82, 85, 90–1, 93, 99; and Bibliography, Appendix 3.
Bannister, George, Private, 31.
Barnard, Anne, the Lady, 50.
Bass, George, 53, 60 and *n*.
Bass Straits, 53, 82, 86, 89, 95.
Batavia, 10, 14, 72, 113.
Bath, 84, 102, 104.
Baudin, Nicolas, Commodore, 65, 85–9, 105.
Beagle, H.M.S., 235 tons, 105.
Becke, George Louis, Bibliography, Appendix 3.
Beethoven, 1.
Bideford, 114.
Bligh, William, Captain, 36, 60, 79, 81, 83, 91–2, 95–6, 99, 100, 102, 118, 121.
Blue Mountains, 77, 105, 121.
Botany Bay, 4, 50, 85, 87–8, 110.
Bounty, H.M.S., 18, 36, 60.
Bounty mutineers, 81; see also *Bounty*, H.M.S.
Bowes, Arthur, Surgeon, 112; and Bibliography, Appendix 3.
Britannia, store-ship, 301 tons, 29, 34, 85.
Brothers, The, ship, 356 tons, 105 *n*.
Bryant, Mary, 18.
Buenos Aires, 97 *n*.
Buffalo, H.M.S., 37, 50, 56, 58, 91–3.

Buffalo diary of voyage, 1807, 96–9, 101.
Buonaparte, *see* Napoleon.
Burford, Mrs., 43.
Burford, Peter Thomas, the Revd., 43–4.
Burrington, Col., 11.
Butler, convict woman, 45, 52.

Calcutta, 28.
Caley, George, 40–2, 91, 119.
Camden, Lord, Secretary of State, 80.
Camden Park, 80, 105–6, 108, 121.
Cape Horn, 83, 95–6.
Cape of Good Hope, 8–13, 18, 36, 39, 45, 49–52, 60, 93, 117.
Cape Town, see Cape of Good Hope.
Cape Verde Islands, 8.
Castle Hill, rebellion at, 68.
Castlereagh, Lord, Secretary of State, 72, 101, 120.
Chapman, Schoolmaster, 114–15.
Chapman, William, 7, 9, 13, 16, 20, 21, 23–4, 26, 29, 33–4, 68–72, 75, 87, 93, 108, 114.
— miniature of, 42; and Bibliography, Appendix 3.
Charlie Tara, aboriginal, 109.
Charlotte, Queen, 30, 107–8, 108 *n*.
China, 12, 77.
Clark, Ralph, Lieut., 20; and Bibliography, Appendix 3.
Coal River, *see* Newcastle.
Collins, David, Judge-Advocate, 15 *n*., 17, 25 *n*., 90, 110; and Bibliography, Appendix 3.
Colnett, James, Captain, 69–72.
Contractor, East Indiaman, 34.
Convicts:
    settlement of, established at Sydney Cove, 3, 4.
    settlement of, established at Norfolk Island, 3–5.
    voyage of First Fleet of, 4.

INDEX

Convicts (*cont.*)
food supplies of, 5, 59.
women, chosen for Norfolk Island, 5, 112–14.
Ann Inett, 5, 113–14.
Third Fleet of, to sail, 8.
at Simon's Bay, 12.
transports at Cape Town, 12.
illness and deaths among Third Fleet, 17.
Mary Bryant and other escapees, 18.
embarked in H.M.S. *Gorgon*, 18.
distribution of, on Norfolk Island, 21.
and the reading of King's Commission, 22.
pardons and marriages of, 22.
and the military, 24, 30–2.
character, health, and hunger of, 24.
King's attitude towards, 25, 32, 68.
production of plays by, 30.
and the Norfolk Island mutiny, 30–2.
as surgeons, 33.
women, carried by *Speedy*, 44–5.
death of, 45, 52.
panic among, 45.
Mrs. King's pity for, 45.
amusements of, 46.
behaviour of, 46–7, 81.
Jane Dundas, 47, 62, 71, 84–5.
reformation of, 50.
and the Lady Anne Barnard, 50.
at Sydney, 55.
and drink, 57, 61.
children of, 57, 63–4.
clothing of, 61.
assignment of, 62, 106, 108.
character of, 62, 65.
emancipated to form bodyguard, 63.
matrimony unusual among, 65–6.
women, treatment of, 66.
political, 66–7.
'General' Joseph Holt, 66.
revolt of, at Castle Hill, 68.
executions of, 68.
Captain Colnett's protégée, 70.

Convicts (*cont.*)
supposed corrupt practices of the Kings concerning, 72–3.
and church-going, 73–5.
church burnt by, 74.
George Howe, 75.
sent to Van Diemen's Land, 76.
settlement of, at Port Phillip, 89.
settlement of, at Hobart, 90.
and the Hannibal Macarthurs, 108.
transportation of, ceases, 108.
loss of cattle by, 118, 121.
as bushrangers, 121.
as jail attendants, 121.
Cook, James, Captain, 26, 35, 38, 60, 86–7, 145.
Coombe, Anna Josepha, 2, 3; *see* King, Anna Josepha.
Cornwall, 111.
Coupang, 18.
Cow Pastures, 119, 121, and Appendix 2.
Crawford, Mrs., 51.
Cuming, *see* Dundas (Mrs. Francis Dundas).

Daedalus, store-ship, 27–8, 49.
d'Artois, Count, 73.
Dawes, William, Lieut., 80.
Decaen, Charles, General, 87.
De Falbe, Emmeline, Mme, 105.
— Journal of, 105–9; and Bibliography, Appendix 3.
Devonshire, 11.
Discovery, H.M.S., 27.
Dundas, Francis, General, 49.
Dundas, Henry, Lord Melville, 50.
Dundas, Jane, 47, 62, 71, 84–5.
Dundas (Mrs. Francis Dundas), 49, 51.
Dunheved (estate), 106, 108, 111.

East Indies, 41.
Edwards, Edward, Captain, 18, and Bibliography, Appendix 3.
Elba, 103.
Eldershaw, M. Barnard, Bibliography, Appendix 3.
Elizabeth Farm, 81.
Endeavour, H.M.S., 35.

125

INDEX

First Fleet, 3, 4, 11, 60, 85, 87, 112.
Flinders, Ann (Mrs. Matthew Flinders), 77–9, 84, 87.
Flinders, Matthew, 53, 77–9, 84–7, 105; and Bibliography, Appendix 3.
France, 1, 26, 76, 82, 87–9, 103, 115.
Franklin, family, 78.
Freame, William, 108 n.
French Explorers, see Baudin, Péron, *Géographe*, *Naturaliste*.
French Fleet, 41, 44, 115.
French vignerons, 60.
Friends of the People, 66.

Géographe, Corvette, 85–6.
George III, 1, 17, 74, 78, 90, 92, 100, 107–8, 108 n.
Gipps, George, Sir, Governor, 105.
Gippsland, 105.
Glatton, H.M.S., 69–71.
Gorgon, H.M.S., frigate, 40 guns, 6–8, 10–18, 22, 27, 34, 49, 55, 104.
Gower, General, see Leveson-Gower, John, Major-General.
Graaf, Mynheer van, 11.
Grant, James, Lieut., 53.
Grenville, Lord, 3, 6.
Grose, Elizabeth, Mrs., see Paterson, Elizabeth, Mrs.
Grose, Francis, Major, 32, 84–5.
Guardian, H.M.S., store-ship, 11, 12.

Hamilton, George, Surgeon, Bibliography, Appendix 3.
Harris, John, Surgeon, 64.
Hatherleigh, 2.
Henslow, John, Sir, 37, 38.
Herschel, Caroline, 1.
Hobart Town, Van Diemen's Land, 90, 100.
Hogarth, 17.
Holt, Joseph, 'General', 66.
Home, Everard, 91.
Horn, Cape, see Cape Horn.
Houston, John, Captain, 97.
Howe, George, 75.
Hunter, John, Governor, 36, 56–9, 61, 73–4, 90–2, 100.

Inett, Ann, 5, 113–14.
Investigator, H.M. sloop, 77, 85–6.
Isle-de-France, 87, 89.

Jacobins, 66.
Java, 72.
Jeffrey, Walter, Bibliography, Appendix 3.
Jenner, Edward, 108.
Jersey, 116.
Johnson, Richard, Revd., 16, 22, 64, 73–4.
Johnson (Mrs. Richard Johnson), 16, 17.

Kangaroo, 4, 16, 18, 90.
Kent, William, Captain, 50, 59, 63, 78, 91.
Kew Garden, 36, 38, 90.
King, Anna Josepha (Mrs. Philip Gidley King):
portraits of, frontispiece and 36.
before marriage, 7.
marriage of, 2–4, 6.
sails for Norfolk Island, 6.
at Teneriffe, 8, 9; St. Jago, 9; Cape Town, 10, 12.
at Sydney, 1791, 15–17.
arrives Norfolk Island, 20–3.
and William Chapman, 20, 23, 26, 33–4, 71, 75.
birth of son of, 23, 111.
birth of daughters of, 26, 33–4, 93, 111.
hostess to Maoris, 26, 28.
illness of, 33.
leaves Norfolk Island, 1796, 34.
arrives in England, 1797, 35.
and the *Porpoise*, 37–42.
and the *Speedy*, 43–5.
sails for N.S.W., 1799, 44.
Speedy diary of, 46–54, 61–2.
arrives Sydney, 1799, 54.
first Governor's Lady, 58.
at Government House, 58–60.
clothing of, 60–2.
and D'Arcy Wentworth, 62.
servants of, 62.
and the Orphanage, 63–6, 79, 88.
and the United Irish, 67–8.

INDEX

King, Anna Josepha (*cont.*)
  gossip concerning, 72.
  and church, 74–5, 107.
  entertaining by, 75–6, 78.
  excursions by, 76.
  and Matthew Flinders, 77–9, 84.
  estranged from Mrs. Macarthur and Mrs. Paterson, 78–82.
  and Mrs. Paterson, 84.
  and Jane Dundas, 47, 62, 84–5.
  and Commodore Baudin, 87–9.
  and the Macarthurs, 92, 95, 101–2, 105, 109.
  and Governor Hunter, 92.
  an amanuensis, 93.
  leaves Sydney, 1807, 93–5.
  character of, 93–4.
  Buffalo diary of, 96–8.
  widowed, 101.
  finances of, 101 and Appendix 3.
  and Captain Piper, 102–3.
  wishes to return to N.S.W., 102–4.
  arrives Sydney, 1832, 104.
  last years of, 105–9.
  death of, 1844, 109.
  children of, 111.
  property of, Appendix 2.
  Bibliography, Appendix 3.
King, Anna Maria, *see* King, Maria.
King, Elizabeth, 34, 36–7, 40, 45, 47, 53, 56, 62, 71–2, 75, 77, 84–5, 89, 102, 104, 111, 115, 118.
King, Harriet (Mrs. P. P. King), 104, 111.
King Island, 86, 88–9.
King, Maria (Mrs. Hannibal Macarthur), portrait, 109; 26, 28, 34, 37, 41, 43–4, 49, 71, 99, 102–5, 109, 111, 114–16.
King, Mary, 93, 104, 111, 118.
King, Norfolk, 34 *n.*, 44, 101, 112–17.
King, Philip Gidley, Governor:
  portraits, 3, 37, 87.
  and Governor Phillip, 3, 32, 36, 93.
  sent to Norfolk Island, 1788, 3.
  visits England, 1790, 3.
  marriage of, 3, 6.
  appointed Lieut.-Governor, Norfolk Island, 4.

King, Philip Gidley (*cont.*)
  children of, 5, 23, 26, 33–4, 71, 75, 111, Appendix 1.
  mentioned, 8–11, 13–15, 17, 20, 53–4, 103.
  arrives Norfolk Island, 1791, 20.
  commission read, 22.
  and William Chapman, 23–4, 33–4, 68–72.
  treatment of convicts by, 25, 68.
  isolation of, 25.
  and the Maoris, 26–9.
  and flax, 26–7, 29.
  and the Norfolk Island mutiny, 30–2.
  and Major Francis Grose, 32, 84.
  ill-health of, 33, 44–5, 91–2, 96, 98–100.
  salary and savings of, 34, 100.
  leaves Norfolk Island, 1796, 34.
  arrives in England, 1797, 35.
  unemployed, 35–6.
  and Sir Joseph Banks, 35–6, 40, 42, 68, 80, 90, 93.
  appointed Governor, N.S.W., 36.
  and the *Porpoise*, 37–42.
  and education of son, Philip Parker, 40, 43–4.
  sails for N.S.W., 1799, 43.
  agent of, 44.
  takes a bath, 45.
  at the Cape, 49–51.
  arrives at Sydney, 1799, 54.
  and Governor Hunter, 56–8.
  and Sydney's social conditions, 57, 60–6.
  and the United Irish, 66–8.
  and the Castle Hill Rebellion, 68.
  duties of, 69.
  and Captain Colnett, 69–72.
  gossip concerning, 72–3.
  and the Church, 73–5.
  and the *Sydney Gazette*, 75–6.
  entertaining by, 76–7.
  excursions by, 76.
  expansion of territory under, 77, 100.
  and Matthew Flinders, 77–8.
  and the Macarthur-Paterson duel, 79.

127

INDEX

King, Philip Gidley (*cont.*)
and John Macarthur, 79, 80, 92, 95.
and Colonel Paterson, 81-4.
and Jane Dundas, 84-5.
and Commodore Baudin, 85-9.
and Port Philip, 86 n., 89.
and Lapérouse, 87-8.
and Van Diemen's Land, 89-90.
and the platypus, 90-1.
hostility of the military to, 91.
succeeded by Bligh, 91.
character of, 92.
sails from Sydney, 1807, 93.
birthday of, 97.
at Rio Janeiro, 99.
arrives in England, 1807, 99.
poverty of, 100.
death of, 1808, 100.
pension for, 100-1.
and the Royal Portraits, 107.
property of, Appendix 2.
Bibliography, Appendix 3.
King, Phillip Gidley, the Younger, 108; and Bibliography, Appendix 3.
King, Phillip Parker, 23, 26, 28, 37, 40, 43, 49, 71, 99, 100, 102-7, 109, 111, 114-15, 118.
King, Port, *see* Port King.
King, Sydney, 44, 101, 112-17.
King, Utricia (infant), 26, 34, 36; 111.
King, Utricia, Mrs., *King Papers*, 43, 75, 114-15.

Lady Juliana, transport, 13.
Lady Nelson, H.M. brig, 60 tons, 53, 86.
Lady Penrhyn, transport, 112.
Lapérouse, 20, 87-8.
Launceston, 111.
Lawrence, Thomas, Sir, 108 n.
Lethbridge, Christopher, 111.
Lethbridge, Harriet, *see* King, Harriet.
Lethbridge, Mary (Mrs. Robert Lethbridge), *see* King, Mary.
Lethbridge, Robert, 104, 111, and Appendix 1.

Leveson-Gower, John, Major-General, 97.
Lisbon, 41.
Louis XVI, 1.
Loyal Associations of Volunteers, 67.
Lymington, 116.

Macarthur, Edward, 95, 102, 109.
Macarthur, Elizabeth (Mrs. John Macarthur), 15, 16, 78-81, 92, 105, 109; and Bibliography, Appendix 3.
Macarthur, Hannibal Hawkins, 102, 105.
family of, 108-9; and Appendix 1.
Macarthur, James (Hannibal), 109.
Macarthur, John, 15, 61, 74, 79-84, 92, 95.
family of, 106, 121.
Macarthur, Maria (Mrs. Hannibal Macarthur), *see* King, Maria.
McKellar, Neil, Lieut., 69.
Macmillan, Surgeon, 98.
Macquarie, Lachlan, Governor, 70, 83, 102, 104, 120-1; and Bibliography, Appendix 3.
Madras, 72.
Maoris, 26-9, 84.
Margate Roads, 39.
Marquis Cornwallis, transport, 34, 114.
Marsden, Elizabeth (Mrs. Samuel Marsden), 95-6.
Marsden, Samuel, Chaplain, 61, 64, 74-5, 80, 95-6, 99, 102, 107.
Mediterranean, 102.
Melbourne, 86, 90.
Merino wool, 48, 61, 74, 80, 99.
Meurant, F., 72.
Minerva, transport, 67.
More, Hannah, 19.
Mozart, 1.
Murray, John, Lieut., 86, 86 n.

Napoleon Buonaparte, 44, 82, 97, 103.
Naturaliste, 350 tons, 86.
Nelson, Lord, 44.

INDEX

Nepean, Evan, Under-Secretary, 3, 24.
Nepean River, 76, 119, 121.
Neptune, transport, 13; and picture, 13.
Newcastle (or Coal River), 55, 66, 100.
New Holland, 1, 6, 8, 14, 35, 53.
New South Wales, *see also* Sydney, N.S.W.:
establishment of settlement in, 3.
supplies for, 11, 12.
mentioned, 27, 107, 112, 114.
Governors of, and Sir Joseph Banks, 36.
King recommended as Governor of, 36.
ships for use of, 37.
plants for, 38, 40–2.
and P. P. King's education, 43.
master-weaver for, 48.
dislikes to be called Botany Bay, 50.
silver Communion service for use in, 74.
first newspaper in, 75.
expansion of, 77, 89, 104–5.
first plough in, 81.
feeling in, 91–2.
and Mrs. King, 93–4.
and Samuel Marsden, 95.
King's civil and naval pay while at, 100.
King's services in, 100.
Mrs. King's property in, 101 and Appendix 2.
and return of P. P. King, 102–4.
and return of Mrs. King, 102–5.
development of, 104–5.
vaccination practised in, 108.
abolition of transportation to, 108.
and Sydney Smith, 110.
land grant in, to Norfolk King, 116–17.
land grants in, to Governor Bligh and King family, 117–18.

New South Wales Corps, 10, 15, 29, 32, 34, 55–6, 63, 67, 69, 81, 84, 92.
and Norfolk Island Mutiny, 32, 34.
New Zealand, 95, 99; and Norfolk Island, 26–9.
New Zealanders, *see* Maoris.
Nile, battle of, 44.
Nootka Sound, 27.
Nore, The, 39.
Norfolk Island:
map, 22.
first settled, 1788, 3, 5, 111–14.
King sent to, 1788, 3, 4.
King appointed Lieut.-Governor of, 4.
description of, 5, 21, 24.
convicts chosen for, 5, 112.
Kings leave Sydney for, 1791, 20.
Atlantic at, 20, 23.
surf and weather at, 20.
Kings and Patersons land on, 1791, 20.
King's Commission read at, 22.
Government House at, 22–3, 58–9.
and William Chapman, 23, 68–9, 71–2.
Mrs. King's children born on, 23, 26, 111.
conditions at, 24–5.
justice at, 24–5.
isolation of, 26.
Kings and Patersons associated on, 26, 81–2.
and Maori visitors, 26–9, 84.
and flax, 26–9.
King's absence from, without leave, 29.
plays performed on, 30–1.
mutiny at, 31–2.
surgeons at, 33.
King's illness on, 33.
King's salary as Lieut.-Governor of, 34.
Britannia at, 34.
King family's departure from, 34.
and shipping communication with Port Jackson, 39, 54.
care of children on, 63–4.

129

INDEX

Norfolk Island (*cont.*)
  banishment of convicts to, 73.
  Mrs. King's affection for, 95.
  mentioned, 110, 111.
  Norfolk King, first child born on, 112–17.
  and Sydney King, 112.
  and Ann Inett, 113–14.
  King's journal of events on, 113; and Bibliography, Appendix 3.
  Norfolk King returns to, and leaves, 114.
  grant of land to Norfolk King on, 116.

Onslow, S. Macarthur, Miss, Bibliography, Appendix 3.
Ornithorhynchus Paradoxus, see Platypus.
Otaheite, 25, 36, 60, 64.
Oxley, John, Lieut., 99.

Pandora, H.M.S., frigate, 18.
Parker, John, Captain, 7, 8, 13, 17, 23.
Parker, Mary Ann, Mrs., 7–19, 113; and Bibliography, Appendix 3.
Parramatta, 55, 64, 67–8, 74–6, 81, 93, 102, 105–7, 109.
Parramatta River, 105–6.
Paterson, Elizabeth (Mrs. William Paterson), 10, 12, 20, 22, 26, 56, 59, 64–5, 67–8, 76, 78–9, 81–5.
Paterson, William, Captain, later Colonel, 10, 12, 20, 26, 55–6, 59, 65, 76, 78–9, 81–5, 89, 91.
Penal Settlement, *see* Convicts.
Péron, François, 65; and Bibliography, Appendix 3.
Peyrouse, *see* Lapérouse.
Phillip (Mrs. Arthur Phillip), 116.
Phillip, Arthur, Governor, 3, 4, 7, 11, 16, 17, 20, 23, 25, 34, 47, 58, 73, 77, 84, 86–7, 90, 93, 100–1, 112, 115–16, 118–19; and Bibliography, Appendix 3.
Phillipsburgh, Norfolk Island, 23.
Piper, John, Captain, 34 *n.*, 102–3; and Bibliography, Appendix 3.

Pitcairn Islanders, 81; see also *Bounty*, H.M.S.
Plate, River, 97 and *n.*
Platypus, 90–1.
Pomarré, Chief, 60.
Porpoise, H.M.S., 37–42, 60, 61, 90.
Port Dalrymple, 100.
Port Jackson, *see* Sydney, N.S.W.
Port King, 86.
Portland, Duke of, 61.
Port Phillip, 86, 89.
Portsmouth, 8, 39, 83.

Queasted, George, Captain of *Speedy* whaler, *see* illustration, 44; 46, 48, 51–4.

Resolution, H.M.S., 38.
Rio de Janeiro, 36, 96, 99.
Riou, E., Lieut., 11.
Ross, Robert, Major, 22.
Rowcliffe, H.M.S., 115.
Rumsey, H. J., Bibliography, Appendix 3.
Runciman, Charles, 104, 111.
Runciman, Elizabeth (Mrs. Charles Runciman), *see* King, Elizabeth.
Russia, 36.

St. Jago, 8, 9.
St. Mary's, *see* South Creek.
Salisbury, Marchioness of, 73.
Savage, John, Surgeon, 108.
Scott, Ernest, Bibliography, Appendix 3.
Second Fleet, 13, 15, 33.
Sheerness, 39.
Sheppard, Captain, 97.
Ships, *see* entries under each name:
  Adventure; Atlantic; Beagle; Bounty; Britannia; Brothers, The; Buffalo; Contractor; Daedalus; Discovery; Endeavour; Géographe; Glatton; Gorgon; Guardian; Investigator; Lady Juliana; Lady Nelson; Lady Penrhyn; Marquis Cornwallis; Minerva; Naturaliste; Neptune; Pandora; Porpoise; Resolution; Rowcliffe; Sirius; Speedy; Thisbe.

130

INDEX

Short, Lieut., and Mrs., 95–7, 99.
Simon's Bay, 10, 12.
Sirius, H.M.S., 80, 87.
Smith, Mrs., 51.
Smith, Sydney, 110.
Society Islands, *see* Otaheite.
South Africa, 8, 9, *see also* Cape of Good Hope, and Bibliography.
South America, 60, 95–7, 111, *see also* Cape Horn.
South Creek, 109, 120.
Spain, 8, 9, 80.
Speedy, whaler, 313 tons; *Speedy* diary, 46–54, 61–2; facsimile of p. 1 of, 44.
Spithead, 4, 6, 8, 113.
Spode, Josiah, 87.
Strzelecki, Paul, Count de, 109.
Subiaco Convent, Parramatta, 106 *n.*
Sydney Bay, Norfolk Island, 21, 112.
Sydney Cove, *see* Sydney, N.S.W.
Sydney Gazette and New South Wales Advertizer, 62 *n.*, 68 *n.*, 75–6, and Bibliography.
Sydney, New South Wales:
 illustrations, 56, 60, 64.
 urgent needs of, 3, 4.
 first days of, 3, 4.
 mentioned, 10–14, 34, 58, 72, 83, 90, 95–6, 112–14, 119.
 hunger at, 13, 14, 113.
 Gorgon at, 15, 104.
 appearance of, 1791, 15, 16.
 sickness at, 17.
 King's Accession and Birthday celebrations at, 17, 78.
 convicts escaped from, 18.
 and Norfolk Island, 25.
 Daedalus at, 27.
 plants for, 38, 41–2.
 Porpoise at, 42.
 Speedy at, 54.
 appearance of, 1799, 55, 58–9.
 jail at, 55, 121 *n.*
 conditions at, 57, 59–67.
 drink traffic at, 57, 61, 69.
 orphanage, 63–5.
 and François Péron, 65.

Sydney, New South Wales: (*cont.*)
 and the Friends of the People, 66.
 and the United Irish, 66–8.
 and the Loyal Association of Volunteers, 67–8.
 and the Church, 67, 73–5.
 Glatton at, 69–71.
 and the *Sydney Gazette*, 75–6.
 Investigator at, 77.
 and Matthew Flinders, 77–9, 84–7.
 Géographe and *Naturaliste* at, 85–6.
 and Baudin, 85–9.
 ill-feeling at, 91–2.
 Governor King leaves, 92.
 Mrs. King's house in, 104.
 Mrs. King returns to, 104.
 The Brothers at, 105.
 and Sydney Smith, 110.
 Mary King born at, 111.
 landing of women convicts at, 113.
Sykes, James, 44.

Table Bay, 12.
Table Mountain, 10.
Tahiti, *see* Otaheite.
Teneriffe, 8, 9, 12.
Third Fleet, 8, 17.
Thisbe, frigate, 97–8.
Trinidad, 45.

Underhill, Lady, 49.
United Irish, 66–8.

Vancouver, George, Captain, 27.
Van Diemen's Land, 53, 76, 83–4, 88–90, 116–17.
Victoria, Queen, 107.
Vienna, 1.
Vineyard, The, 105–9; and picture, 106.

INDEX

Wales, Princess of, 19.
Watteau, 17.
Waterloo, Battle of, 102.
Wentworth, D'Arcy, 33, 62.
West Indies, 7, 36, 41.
Whitelocke, John, Lieut.-General, 97–8.
Whitlock, General, *see* Whitelocke, John, Lieut.-General.
Wild Cattle, 102, and Appendix 2.

Wilkins, W. H., 50 *n.*; Bibliography, Appendix 3.
Wise, Edward, weaver, 48, 61.
Witt, Peter de, 10, 11, 13.
Witt, Peter de, Mrs., 11, 13.
Worcestershire, 113.
Worgan, G. B., Surgeon, 80.

York, Duke of, 69.
Yorkshire, 114.
Young, George, Sir, 49, 50.